CONSUMED

By Emily Robinson

*for the ones I love
who helped me through the most difficult times,
and for the ones who relate*

The slogan of Hell: Eat or be eaten.
The slogan of Heaven: Eat and be eaten.
— W. H. Auden

Prologue

Natalia's brainholes were haunted by Amber's memories. She couldn't live like this. Knowing what she'd done—what Amber had wanted. What she felt she had to do. She couldn't stop remembering. The taste, and everything she lived through.

She tried to stay focused on the concrete. Focused on the traffic: people and passing cars. Natalia had never been to New York before, but she recognized places. Not tourist attractions or major landmarks—she recognized Amber's therapist's office. Her favorite park bench. Her apartment building. They felt like frozen memories, etched into her brain.

Natalia swallowed some pooled-up spit and sat down on the park bench when she realized it wasn't the traffic she was seeing, it was just the color purple. Not quite haze, more a mist. Maybe a state of pure empathy. She was remembering what her own body had never known.

Part I

Amber devoured all the cost-comparing flight content she could find. She was going to use her babysitting money to flee the country.

She stared at the computer screen, which burned her eyeballs, imprinting her retina with the memory of light. Amber wasn't sure how to get herself interested in normal. The stupid things like chilling and going out or watching a movie. She wasn't sure she would ever want to really know another person again. She couldn't breathe, and wanted to cry even though she didn't.

She had taken her independence for granted. At school, she had missed the comforts of home: her duvet, a warm bath with lavender Epsom salt, her mother's shakshuka.

What she hadn't missed were her mother's remarks about her ever-fluctuating weight and her vast or lacking consumption of foodstuffs. Her father telling her how she "should really get out there. Get a job, and work. Get a taste of what the real world is like, so you'll appreciate how special college is" or, at the very least, "Go out and be young! You'll never be this young again. Look! See? You're already older!"

How she craved to feel her slippery youth: time as endless, boredom as free. She didn't smoke, but she loved the smell of it. Like thick wool coats and whiskey, fires and friends. It smelled like death: cozy, inevitable.

She didn't care for crowded spaces. They used to catalyze her anxiety attacks. She liked staying inside and reading and going to bed by 11pm. A nightclub or even a bar often led to panic.

"Have you met anyone you like?" Her father would ask her.

To which Amber would always laugh and say, "Dad, I'm not, like, a loser? You've met my friends."

For a while her parents pestered her, asking if there was something she wanted to tell them.

"What are you even talking about? No." Though, of course, there had been many things she wanted to tell them.

Amber's parents met in college. At Princeton. And now that Amber was in college, at Princeton, no less—well, they wanted her to have what they had, even if they understood how unreasonable their desire was. They wanted her to find love at school, but Amber hadn't so much as mentioned a boy since she and her high school boyfriend had broken up. And everyone knew high school boyfriends didn't count; they were accessories.

Amber's parents simply wanted to make sure she didn't waste her youth. But Amber hated being young. She couldn't wait to be thirty, or forty, sixty-three-and-a-half, one hundred and two. To become one of the invisible people, aged past eroticism. Erased from sight, to be unseen, forgotten, and ignored.

When she was little, she would joke about wanting to be a dog or a cat. How they had it made. Had people trained perfectly. Got all the attention. Had food delivered to them, right on schedule. Slept all day and did nothing but watch TV.

But Amber would kill herself if she were a dog or a cat. The thought of eating nothing but kibble—or worse, that stinky, stringy, slimy pink-brown wet cat food.

Amber pulled out some hair from the very center of her scalp. She had a tuft of broken hair right there, and she kept grasping for it whenever she needed to busy her hands. Her mother hated the hair-pulling and even purchased some Cookie-Monster-blue stress putty.

"You're gonna give yourself a bald spot if you keep doing that. It's disgusting."

Perhaps if she had a bald spot people wouldn't notice her. Or they would notice her enough to stop noticing.

If she could, Amber would be a wall painted nondescript grey. Paint isn't like wallpaper. It can't be removed completely. No matter how much sanding down, they would still be forced to cover her with white to clear the slate before the next shade splayed atop her. She would haunt the walls and infuse the room with her very essence. This was what she wanted instead of a body.

She imagined leaving her own dead carcass, with its heart still miraculously pumping, at the local fire station. Perhaps they could find some use for it. Let her sustain their Dalmatians. Did fire stations even have Dalmatians anymore? Did they ever, or was that just a manufactured construct to create some desired image?

Amber stopped believing in free will in the 11th grade when she read every Brian Greene book McNally Jackson carried. She believed in neurotransmitters and biological reactions that led to patterned behavior. She was nothing if not her body, and her body was evidence.

She made sure she ate three meals every day, and even made sure that she went outside every day, at least once. To be with the elements, which people always pretend don't exist inside.

She thought of her body as a fleshbag, better if left on its own to age and rot. Whenever she left the apartment, she was reminded she could be perceived. She would growl at the next person who talked to her without any encouragement.

Escaping New York would be helpful. Perhaps away from here she could begin to become a person again.

The webpage, blasting blue light, worked on her like caffeine, and the chatter, coming from her mother's book club in the other room, brought her back to the moment.

Amber was relieved when her mother had told her she could hide in her bedroom for the evening, excused from showing face, teeth—smiling plastically—and awkwardly hugging her parents' lumpy friends who liked scarves and the crossword and smiled too much. Each of these gatherings felt like the other.

She grabbed her phone, opened Twitter, and loaded her newsfeed, barely processing her own actions.

@iconiqueboibish: bachelor in paradise is how dating works

@edithwhoreton: lol just had to convince my godmother that my generation wasn't mad at her for being a cis straight woman

> **@lacroixifixion:** have to gag

@iconiqueboibish: also im on tinder, raya, grindr, hinge, and bumble, who wants to be my sugar daddy and bankroll me onto the league??? venmo me @iconiqueboibish

@edithwhoreton: tbh writing emails out of indignation is my kink

@drappleistheog: Love when the world thinks ur a pushover

> **@drappleistheog:** and the second ur not, ur a bitch

@lacroixifixion: just texted someone"I was more—it was a bit. but--"

@drappleistheog: I—

When Amber was little she used to cut up words into bits and pieces. She knew new ew e how ow o to o break them hem he e and an a tried to o see how ow o far fa a she he e could break them before they hey he e had ha a lost all meaning. She he e did this his is to o pass ass as the he time, and to soothe her he mind from fro anxious thoughts thought though hough. It's how ow she he coped cope cop.

When hen Twitter and text txt talk became a language, she knew new ew it was wuz her time 2 fly. No 1 could tell her he she he wuz wrong any more bc wat wuz her mind wat wuz spellcheck what did she do on accident—and who cared ??? and wat did she do on purpose? Intent was dead and deceased rip her phone had died. It died die di—

She clicked back to the Norwegian Air website and compared their flight offerings for various destinations. Her mouth was slick.

The cost of the flights to Germany were comparable to the cost of the flights to Italy which were comparable to the costs of flights to Alicante, Bardufoss, Cyprus, and Kirstiansand. Did she want to trip in Amsterdam? Or stuff herself with beer and bratwurst? Did she want to join a cult in Sweden? Or eat nothing but baguettes? She Googled hostels in Madrid, Barcelona, Rome, and Berlin. She wanted to stay forever. As long as she could afford to stay, and for as long as summer would last her. She wanted to become one with some other city.

But why was everything so goddamn expensive? She had money saved, but even hostels were so expensive. Plus train fares?? Forget food—museums. Where were there couches on which she could crash? And then she remembered that party she went to last semester with the ultimate frisbee team, that hippie who had graduated the year prior—yet was still awkwardly living on their mutual friend's couch?? He had worked on a farm for room and board. In Portugal, was it? She did some investigative Googling and found the site that facilitated his fucking off all summer long in Europe.

She clicked around its Very Official Sounding website until her fears of over-laborious labor and unsafe accommodations were quelled. She filled out the application: No, she was not a felon; no, she had never been convicted of a crime involving violence or sexual (mis)conduct; no, she had never been required to register as a sex or drug offender; nope, no, never-ever arrested or convicted for causing physical or emotional injury to any person or property; yes, she agreed to their terms and conditions; and, yes, she would enter her credit card number and pay the application fee.

Charlie was working as a paralegal in Memphis all summer; she should be out having some magical experience working on a farm in the European countryside. She could get ripped from the manual labor. Maybe she would even meet a hot farmhand and, like, travel even more till school started back up.

Amber submitted her application and loaded Netflix. She watched three and a half episodes of some new comedy about being young and skinny in a new city. And Amber felt empty inside. She could never watch new content at night when trying to will herself to sleep. She always got too invested in finishing the binge and finding out how things ended. Especially when it was predictable.

Once her eyes lost their will to watch, Amber shut her computer screen and snuggled deeper into the sheets. She closed her eyes.

Two minutes passed, but felt like fifteen. Amber grabbed her phone and scrolled through Instagram and Twitter. And Instagram again, just one last time. She put her phone back on the side table and shut her eyes. Then opened her eyes, rolled to her side, and grabbed her phone. She wasn't positive she had set her alarm.

She had.

A text from Emma popped up:

> U awake?

> yee

> what's up

> allie and I r going to 3$bill pull thru

> im in bed

                                          have fun

                                          luv u

She dreamt of everything she was missing:

    The Frick Collection pre-renovation.

    China Chalet with Laney and her hot, coke-addicted Eurotrash friends.

    Charlie's face. Like the Joker's. Smile carved into his flesh.

Amber awoke early the next morning to her iPhone buzzing. She silenced it and checked her notifications. There were a bunch of random texts she ignored, opting first to flip through her finsta feed.

The day prior she posted a photo of herself pouting into a mirror looking like "skintyyyyyyyyy twink goals." "y didn't u rinsta??" "love this!"

She checked her emails. Mostly junk: Glossier, Google Alerts, Free People, Gilt, Teen Vogue, AllPosters, Gap, and Lena at Delish. And an email approving her application. She rolled over from her back, on to her stomach, collecting more covers beneath her body as she reached for her computer and made her way to the website.

She scrolled through all the listings and sent out 47 emails to different farms in sleep-hazy mania. She shut her computer and got out of bed.

Her mother and father were in the kitchen, pretending to be the Photoshopped version of themselves—a schtick started in the wake of Amber's Panic Attack on 57th and 10th. She almost missed the meaningless bickering that had become the soundtrack to her daily life.

The Panic Attack on 57th and 10th came after seeing some off-Broadway play she begged her mother to take her to, about the bleakness of life and the inevitability of continued hopefulness in the face of reason.

"What'd you think?" Amber asked.

The edge of her mother's lips sagged down toward the ground before she said, "It was a little depressing."

"Yeah, it made me feel like a hamster on one of those—." Amber gesticulated.

"Wheels!" Her mother said.

Amber placed her right index finger and middle finger onto her neck, and articulated each breath.

"Are you alright?"

"Yeah, sorry."

"Are you sure?"

Amber nodded, yes, but her feet betrayed her and stopped moving. "I feel like I'm having a heart attack even though, of course I know I'm not." They went to the nearest urgent care where Amber told the doctor, "I know I'm not having a heart attack but I feel like—I know it's anxiety. I know—can you please do an EKG? I'm sorry."

She wanted to disappear and she couldn't stop herself from crying. It was so stupid. She knew it was all in her head but she couldn't turn it off. She hadn't been to urgent care for a false alarm since high school. This felt like regression. She understood she couldn't control the world, but why couldn't she control her mind?

The urgent care doctor gave her a prescription for five days' worth of Xanax and advised her to see a therapist, saying it was quite surprising that she had never seen one before, considering her recurrent displays of extreme panic.

It had taken her till the age of 12 to be able to swallow a pill, but Amber ate the Xanax prescribed to her, day by day, for five days straight, and felt nothing. Good-nothing. Normal-nothing. She felt like Amber. It was weird that people got high on Xanax, when it just made her normal.

When Amber was little and got sick, her mother had to hide her medication in peanut butter. It seldom worked, so they just wound up buying chewables and gummy vitamins until she started Accutane in high school for her acne. She hadn't believed she could manage the daily pills and monthly blood tests, but her desire to clinically airbrush her face won out. She swallowed the extreme dosage of Vitamin A that made up Isotretinoin for months, and signed a waiver ensuring she would always use at least two forms of birth control. High levels of Vitamin A can legitimately fuck up a baby. It can lead to the formation of a cleft palate, heart defects, eye and ear abnormalities, fluid in the brain, a very small head, facial dysmorphism, nervous system malformations, and intellectual disabilities.

Amber imagined herself as her own Accutane baby all grown up.

She had selected no sex and condoms, even though having no sex seemed like a pretty effective means of not getting pregnant all on its own.

Amber hated allowing a foreign agent to influence her insides, but now she was able to swallow pills. After the Xanax ran out, she went to see a medical therapist, who prescribed her propranolol.

Propranolol was technically a blood pressure medication, which Amber found to be quite concerning. When she was younger and had panic attacks, she hadn't realized they were panic attacks. She thought she had low blood pressure and claustrophobia. But still, what if the blood pressure medication actually gave her low blood pressure? All this talk of blood pressure made it shoot up.

Amber's medical therapist referred her to a selection of talk therapists as supplement to the propranolol. She found the talk therapy to be somewhat helpful. She liked having a sounding board: someone to validate and occasionally question what she said. But she mostly felt like her mind went in so many circles that she'd already had the conversations she'd have with her therapist, on her own.

Coffee was brewed, and oranges were squeezed into a pulpy juice.

"How was book club?" Amber remembered to ask her mother.

"Lorene drank too much again; she thinks Brad is seeing someone already. It's only been a month since he filed which means, well, who knows," her mother said as her father scoffed, shaking his head.

He offered, "Orange juice? I can make eggs. Just got some fresh ones from the farmer's market."

"I'm not super hungry. Also, I just wanted you to know, it won't, like, cost you anything or—I might go to Italy?"

That quieted the room.

"What do you mean? Why?!" Amber's mom asked.

"I just—I dunno. I just thought?"

"That sounds great, sweetie." Amber's dad finally spoke up.

"Sure. Fine. How are you gonna pay for—Italy?"

"Yeah. So, I guess I was, like, thinking about how I'm not really doing anything here. And I thought a change of— it could be good. You know? I've been doing some, like research, and I think I could work on a farm for room and board. And I have some money saved from babysitting."

"You want to work on a farm in Italy?" her mom asked.

"Or a vineyard. I sent emails to vineyards mostly."

"For how long?" Amber's mother asked, on offense.

"Maybe a month? Till school starts?" Amber continued, "There's this website. I know people who have—it's like a meme? When people say they wanna quit college—"

"You're not quitting college."

"No, I'm not—I would just be doing it for—but when people are tired of academia, we're like, oh maybe I'll just go, like, work on a farm for a while."

"What is it exactly?" Her mom asked.

"So, it's like this website that certifies and connects workers with hosts and basically you get room and board in exchange for labor on sustainable farms."

"You're telling me you're gonna be a farmhand?"

"I mean, yeah."

Amber's father said, "I think it's great. She should do manual labor at some point in life."

"Exactly! Plus, I can practice and, like, actually learn Italian." This silenced her mother.

"I'm not doing anything here. I've applied to so many jobs, and I don't have an internship, and I feel like I'm just wasting all my time."

"Well, you will need to find a job at some point."

"I've tried? And I haven't gotten any yet? And what I'm doing is kind of a job!" Amber continued, "In Italy. I would be working. Actually working."

By the time she returned to her room, coffee in hand, an email awaited her attention: Podere Condito had room for her, whenever she could get there. Amber immediately confirmed her interest, asking how best to coordinate the particulars. Her stomach didn't feel like her stomach; it felt like a dance floor, full of bops and vomit. Holyfuckingshit.

She reopened the Norwegian Air webpage and searched for the cheapest flights to Rome, the city closest to Trevinano, home to Podere Condito.

She began the check-out process for a flight that left in three days. The website mistook her for a bot when she accidentally selected a streetlight-adjacent image which, itself, contained no streetlights. After five screens of photographs cut up into nine boxes, she convinced the Are You a Bot? question-machine that she was a human.

A seat on the Tuesday 1:30PM EST flight from JFK to FCO was hers.

She could scream. But instead, she channeled her energy into obsessively Google stalking Podere Condito: they had 428 likes on Facebook, all 5-star reviews, they seem to enjoy jam-making, and their wine sold for forty-eight euros a pop.

"You're going to Italy?" her therapist repeated.

Amber took her therapist's disdain quite personally. She picked at her cuticle. "Yeah. I just—yeah."

"Can we unpack that?"

"I've actually been doing more packing than unpacking." Amber smiled with her mouth, but not with her eyes. "I—yeah, no. I know I'm running away."

"Go on—."

"No, yeah, I—"

Her therapist cocked her head.

"I don't know what to say. Like yeah, I want to escape the city," Amber said.

"Why do you think that is?"

"What do you mean? You know how shitty this summer has been."

Her therapist nodded.

"I just—I think. I finally soft-blocked—"

"What?"

"Like, blocked and unblocked—basically forced them to unfollow me."

"Okay, I see."

"But I soft-blocked Charlie, but also Laney and Robby. But because I soft-blocked, sometimes I still check their profiles, since they're public and they haven't blocked me?"

"All right?"

"And Laney and Robby are in New York this summer, so—it's just—

you know."

"Uhuh—."

"It's, like, I shouldn't have to leave. But I also don't want to be anywhere near them."

"So, you're leaving because of them."

"Yeah. But also, because what else am I doing? I can't get hired at The Strand even though I'm halfway finished with an English degree from Princeton. Not that that makes me more qualified, I just—well, I guess on paper I think it maybe should make me qualified. Did you know—there's like a test? It's like applying to college, they have, like, essay questions you have to answer? I wrote them this whole—essay on—." Amber's fiery eyes caught the deadened gaze of her therapist and her rage-speckled enthusiasm was squashed and replaced with her best mask of calm. "I'm not sure why I—my mom said instead of going to Italy I should get a job. Which is true. And I'm not making money in Italy. But I will be working. So, that's something. Laney, Charlie, and Robby are applying for Fulbrights but maybe I'll be able to say more than mi chiamo Amber and burrata in Italian come September. 'Cause those are—comparable things. You know? I don't know. I just need to escape New England. Get closer in proximity to England-England."

"Does Manhattan count as New England?"

"Doesn't it?"

"Does it?"

"Doesn't matter. It was a joke. Don't worry, I'm not pursuing a career in comedy."

"I still don't understand why you're going to Italy."

"I'm learning Italian? So, I guess thought it'd be fun, but also maybe I'd actually learn to like speak Italian."

"How long have you been learning Italian?"

"Why?"

"No reason, just curious."

"Just since last year. I'm not great at it," Amber said.

"All right. So, you're going to Italy to become fluent?"

"Maybe not fluent, but it'd be nice to be able to say what I mean." Amber looked into her lap and folded one leg over the other.

"Do you think you can say what you mean in English?"

"I—know that I can't? But we have to grasp for—I want to. I know I can't, but I understand how to—try?"

"All right. Well, I guess I will see you—"

"I should be back, like, mid-August for a few weeks before school starts."

Amber's therapist asked, "Same time?" Amber nodded, and so her therapist continued, "shall we mark Monday, August 19th? 2:45?"

"Yeah, that should—actually, you know, let's do the week after. Just in case—"

"So, the 26th?"

"Yeah, that's—let me—" Amber grabbed her backpack and pawed around till she found her planner. She marked down the appointment, and also made a note to let Emma know she'd be gone for the rest of summer. She'd probably be relieved, honestly. Amber hadn't been much fun.

Amber had packed and unpacked, repacked, unpacked, and packed again—guessing which shoes and jeans should suffice in the fields, how much shampoo, conditioner, and toothpaste she might need. She had chosen not to bring her meds as she feared being stopped for drug trafficking at the border, but she did bring along bandaids and Compeed, her preferred brand of blister-specific bandaids. Everything was in order: her passport was pulled and she had snacks prepped. Cashews, 2 Kind bars, and a 70% dark chocolate bar. There was nothing left to do but overthink what was already done and planned.

Going to bed early made the morning feel closer. It'd be cute to say she dreamt of Tuscan adventures, but she had a nightmare in which she and Charlie were babysitting Julianne Moore's daughter?? The house itself started haunting them.

She woke with fright at 5:26AM. Did Julianne Moore even have a child? Amber wasn't sure, so she unplugged her phone and Googled: "Julianne Moore daughter." She was oddly delighted to discover that Moore did, indeed, have a daughter with Bart Freundlich, named Liv Freundlich. Liv was a teenaged-girl who TheFamousPeople.com identified as both "an American actress and activist." She wasn't sure why her hunger for the flesh of her ex-friend melded with this horror of the home. She wouldn't be able to ask her therapist until the end of August. Maybe she'd simply seen Liv and Julianne in some Buzzfeed article about famous celebs with their lookalike kids. In before times she would have texted Charlie about this.

Googled images of Podere Condito popped back into her mind. She must be nervous, she told herself, nervous that their home will not feel like one to her.

She gave up on any hope for returning to slumber and decided, instead, to embrace this obscene hour for consciousness and fresh oxygen, and maybe even surround herself with trees and green.

Amber waded through the thick summer air, heading crosstown toward Central Park West. She had this crushing urge to text Charlie and make sure he was okay, even though she didn't want him to be. Thinking of him always made her more depressed. She wished she could be another person, have another body, to go and right the wrongs she, herself could never un-wrong. She tried to stop thinking, re-thinking, over-thinking the past, and force her thoughts—.

A slobbering pug surprised her with a wet, coarse tongue on her calf. Its owner apologized as Amber knelt down to pet him. They locked eyes, Amber and the pug. Oxytocin flooded her mindholes.

The owner led the pug away and Amber stood alone staring at the park, an intersection away. The pedestrian light had switched to Walk. She couldn't move. Her feet wouldn't step forward. The eggshell-color of Charlie's walls is all she could see. Her feet stood on the manmade sidewalk. Charlie yelling at her. The air slapped. Her chest contracted. Crying in the cab at three in the morning as Emma held her, consoling. She tried to focus on her breath, the air, her blouse on her skin, the sounds. A firetruck passed. Her chest felt tight. She moved her right middle and pointer fingers to the left side of her neck, feeling for her pulse. Her heartbeat like it always did.

She moved her fingers to her nose, covered one nostril, and breathed through the other. She held her breath, holding in the nothingness.

Her thought-stream slowed. She inhaled through the other nostril. Maybe this was why she hated running so much: her mind ran marathons so her body didn't have to. Maybe she'd be happier if her body did the work instead.

At the frisbee team party, the fuck-off-and-farm-guy had asked her how her anxiety manifested itself. Like, what did it feel like? He had never felt it before. The overwhelming narcissism of self-interested worry. He wasn't crippled by his own existence. Who was this neurotypical specimen? She couldn't recall his name. Was it Jay? Chadwick? Grayson??? She wracked her brain trying to remember everything she was forgetting. All the little nothings that blurred into other nights of nothings. Her mind wouldn't leave the party.

The light had switched from Walk to Stop back to Walk again. Amber willed her legs forward, one then the next. She sat down on a bench, ditching her effort to enter the park in favor of rest and dealing with the capering of her stomach and mind. Maybe she did believe in free will.

It had been the first time she'd seen him, after everything. She and Emma were chilling by the drinks, then Emma got distracted. Amber wound up wasting time with the nameless fuck-off-and-farm-guy, ignoring the Charlie-shaped hole on the other end of the room. There he was with his smug smile—they didn't make eye contact or anything. She worried he would ruin her life. That he would cancel her publicly, ruin her future. She wasn't sure how he possibly could. What he could say she had done. But this what she feared.

Amber pulled out her phone and opened Instagram. She searched @Char1ieB3ar47 and searched for content yet unseen by her. There was one "friend appreciation post" celebrating Laney, which featured photos of both of them together at bars and traipsing around the city. She kept scrolling through the selection of photos and noticed that she had taken one of the later shots. She clicked on Laney's face to find her handle, jumping to her profile.

The only content new to Amber was a photo of Laney with three other girls with Drybar Mai Tai blow-outs, in front of the Klondike bar dessert at Catch with the caption "I thought this happened years ago??? Happy 21st Gracie!!!!" Amber zoomed in on the photo. Laney was smizing. Gracie's eyes were mid-blink.

Amber x-ed out of @bluestonelaney's profile and searched @PiuOMenoRobby. There was a photo of him dressed as a cowboy. Amber rolled her eyes, which were now salty, coated by the formation of tears. She blinked. And took a breath.

Her mind was back to sprinting. At Emma's pregame they were talking shit about Robby and Laney. About how Laney was a Zionist and how Robby wanted to be Ben Affleck.

"I want a refill." Emma said.

They made moves for the kitchen.

"It's like, come on, like, have even a bit of a backbone. You know? Like with Laney and Robby."

"I mean, yeah. They're just bottoms and Charlie's—. Also, Laney's just stupid."

"Emma!"

"No, I'm telling you! I took that Virginia Woolf class with her last year, and she's literally—like, Professor Mandlebaum hated her. He called her Dana all semester.'"

"King."

"Mandlebaum fucks. I'm like, adopt me, sir. Please? Or can I adopt him as my father?"

"It's so crazy, though. Thinking about how like, I mean you remember? Last winter break when Charlie was on that ski trip? He was literally Skyping me for hours for emotional support even though he was on the trip with Laney and Robby!"

"No, I mean, we know this. Charlie sucks."

"He's drinking again."

"Did he ever stop?"

"He was counting his drinks for a while. But I mean, he's twenty-three years old. Like, I don't care he's in college. He's been drinking since he was what? Like thirteen? He's an adult. How many interventions does it take?"

"I can't believe you held an intervention for that shithead."

"We were friends."

"Oh, I remember." Emma paused, then added, "God. Remember formal?"

Amber hated remembering Emma's formal. "Yeah."

"He blacked out at the pre-game. You didn't even make it to Winberie's."

"I know."

"You love Winberie's!"

Amber said, "I do."

Emma softened, "It's not on you."

"It's just kind of scary. You think you know a person—."

"Tonight's should be fun, though," Emma said as she poured herself more whiskey and Coke.

A car blasting Kanye sped down the street, jolting Amber back from nostalgifying. She wiped her cheek dry and texted Emma:

                                                                      miss u luv

                                                                          also !!!!!!

im going to italy to work on a vineyard??? all v last minute

                                                                       gonna miss u

                                                  prob won't be back till school

                                                                           but idk

                                      don't have my return tkt yet

                                                                               lol

                               luv being a spontaneous bish

She opened Twitter. Emma and her girlfriend had been tweeting about how they had made a GCal event for the group sex they were having with these boring NYU lesbians. This made her think of Charlie and how he felt so morally superior for being a bisexual man. He only ever dated men, but he liked fucking with women for the clout and power. He was a white, cis, fiscally conservative gay. Hardly a radical identity, which didn't make it inherently bad, though it would have been nice if he could stop talking for five seconds about how difficult it was for him. Anyway! Amber put her phone away and watched the cars, bathing in their passing fluorescence.

She hated this. How she couldn't stop thinking of Charlie. She still felt so manipulated, gullible. It's been a month since the end of the semester, and three months since they'd been close. She should be able to move on. It's just that she felt stupid for not being able to read the signs right in front of her. For falling for his performance. For not seeing how he pretended to be everyone's best friend. How strategically he garnered sympathy when he deserved none.

Sometimes Amber worried that she made it all up. That she hadn't felt pressured or coerced, even when she knew she had.

Because she hadn't said no. She said, "I don't think this is—" She hadn't known what to say. Their relationship felt so fragile suddenly, and she hadn't wanted to break this bond they'd built.

His birthday party was thirteen days after it happened. They hadn't spoken, but they had been texting. Virtually playing pretend.

                  like that wasn't how anything was supposed to go

                                      I just think I need space?

I'm just a little shocked honestly

we've made out before

                                                      I know

liek, we're friends you could have said something

*liek

*like

but you know what I mean?

I just don't want to feel like shit

                           I don't want to feel like shit either

                             I don't want either of us to

                             this is gonna sound stupid

just say it

                      do u not want me to come to your party?

                                     you know me

                 if I don't ask I'll worry u don't want me there

                        Or I'll spiral before I get there

               and think ur mad at me for not being there

you're my best friend

this is just

a lot

of course you should be there

Ok

really gonna ok me?

Okay

okayyyyyyyyyyyy*

no lol ur not allowed to make a tfios reference

I reject this

Charlie grew up in town, so instead of going out, he kicked his parents out of their home for his "birthday shindig."

Amber's plan was to make an appearance. Be polite, stay for an hour or two. Stay mostly sober but performatively sip a Solo cup filled with Trader Joe's Two Buck Chuck red blend. Stick with Emma but engage in the required small talk with the familiar cast of randoms.

An hour and some minutes in, he approached. She couldn't tell how plastered he was. He had a knack for seeming sober while being blacked.

"Can we talk?" he asked. He must have been long gone. But it was his birthday.

"Charlie, of course. Literally, anytime."

He pulled her into his bedroom, his childhood bedroom, with the eggshell walls etched over with pencil marks displaying his physical growth. His walls were not relaxing; they felt like drowning in mayonnaise. She tried not to suffocate.

She hated that he had all the Percy Jackson books. He weirdly still always talked about his signed copies. They were in college, why did he still care that Rick Riordan wrote the words "To Charlie" one time?

Amber wanted to be Annabeth so bad when she was younger, but only because she wanted to be like Athena.

They were on the shelf right next to Eragon. She didn't want to think of Charlie as a teenager right then while he was yelling at her. Screaming so loud two people knocked on the door to ask if everything was all right.

His dream catcher had beads and no feathers. A Family Guy poster was pasted onto the wall. Twelve souvenir snow globes and six shot glasses were lined up on the desk.

His bloodshot eyes. Must be crossed. His glasses reflected her image back at her. Her heels dug in to his fluffy, cream rug.

He was mad at her for making him this angry, for making it impossible to control his temper. He had been so good! He had been working on his temper. He had it under control until he didn't.

But he wasn't a predator. He couldn't be. He, himself, had been abused before, and so to call him a predator was an act of violence. Amber was committing violence against him.

"I'm sorry, Charlie. I didn't mean to—"

"But you knew? Do you know how much that hurts? What a fucking betrayal that was?"

"I never called you a predator." Never to his face. All she had said was she needed some space. He had pushed her head down that night, when they had just gone to his room to get space and watch The Goldbergs. After she had said no, he put his hand to her head and used force to guide it toward his groin and she felt—yeah, that's it really, I mean, she just, she felt pressured. And she didn't know how to say no again. And she didn't know how to be his friend anymore.

At his birthday party, he yelled at her for this. He told her how much her texts offended him. And hadn't they kissed before? And she said yes, sure they had. But it was college. People kiss. It's all fun and ridiculous, performative nonsense. It's all games until you're not playing because you want to. You're playing because there's a gun to your head, a cock to your mouth. In your mouth. And you gag. And you want to bite down and castrate him. But instead, it chokes you, and you want to throw up and you feel like you can't ever speak again. It'd be great if you threw up. Throw up on his dick, Amber willed herself. Created friction between her vocal cords; a sound check, to see if she had lost her voice in all the noise. She shoved the dick deeper in trying to gag herself and throw up on his dick. But she didn't. She just sucked. It sucked.

Charlie claimed that because he was so intoxicated the night that it happened—.

Charlie tried to blame her.

Amber helped lead an intervention for him that fall, with a bunch of their friends. He said there was nothing wrong. He began counting his drinks, but after five he'd start to forget. But he said he didn't have a problem; he was just having fun. But because he was blacked out. Because he was gone. Because he was letting off steam. Charlie said. He said. He yelled at Amber. He told her he couldn't have. He couldn't have because. If anything, I mean. She took advantage of him. He should be—he could be—he could accuse her. If he wanted to. Her stomach gasses rose to her throat, tempting her with the possibility of sweet release. Her body was ill; she had to throw up. She couldn't throw up. All this life was stuck inside her. It lived in her body and would never escape it. She heard everything as nothingness and it was so loud she had to scream, but her scream was silent. It was a gasp. She needed air.

She unconsciously grabbed the side of her torso, half-hugging herself, half-feeling herself up to see how fat or skinny she was. Her skin felt like it had lost collagen. Like she was growing, aging. But she was young, like her dad always reminded her. She was young in this body, even though she wasn't. The world had seen her youth and sucked its sap right out of her, filling her instead with one shitty man. "Gag me," they used to say to each other in jest whenever anyone said or did something particularly cursed or heinous. But then one day he broke the joke? He undid his belt, and unzipped his jeans. He was hard underneath his dinosaur-themed boxers. He pulled his boxers down, and nudged himself closer to her head, which he held in place, firmly grasped between his hands. She was a petulant baby being force-fed from a bottle. But she wasn't so young anymore so instead of forcing nutrients and calories down her throat, he was forcing down his cum. He wanted her to swallow. She closed her eyes, and imagined she was nowhere. In the land of grainy greyness. Dissolved from the responsibilities of corporeality.

She pulled away and said that she should really go home now. He was already under the covers and the sheets, dozing off to sleep.

She stopped being young in her own skin when she came to hate the weight of her own person. She used to take up space like it cost nothing. Her mind soared and sunk on her own body's objectification. Sometimes she had even liked being catcalled, performing as a fetish object. But now she wished to wreck her body, to make it her own site of ruins. A place for worship with its wreckage.

She hated her body because it would not lie to her about where it had been. Her body was evidence. She was born with it, she was given her body, stuck with it without her consent. And yet, she had made her body. Remade her body. She broke her body. She was Shelley, the doctor, and his monster.

She imagined eating the whole wide world. Becoming and deforming it.

Except the whole world was just his dick. And she could swallow the whole world whole. A snake consuming an egg, whole. Piercing it to squeeze out its innards, then upchucking its shell. But she felt like a shell, with her insides all scrambled up. She wanted to eat him, not his cum, but his whole cock. She wanted to eat him just so she could spit him back out.

Laney and Robby took Charlie's side, which was humiliating and made Amber feel crazy. She almost believed his story more than she trusted her memory. She had placed her trust in him, and now she just felt all alone. Like she'd done something wrong and this was her punishment.

The sun peered through the park's foliage. Amber checked her phone. It was 6:47AM by then. A bead of sweat rolled down her back.

She went back home, where she checked her phone. Emma had responded.

> WHAT?!!!!!
>
> OMG
>
> jealous
>
> where in italy???
>
> So hot
>
> im so fuxked up rn Angel brought coke n Aydan had ket
>
> I'm so crszd realizing lots
>
> wow

Her parents were awake now. Coffee brewed.

"How do you feel, world traveler?" Her dad said.

She rolled her eyes and said something cutesy to appease him. They quietly consumed eggs and bacon while Amber didn't think of Charlie and her mother finished making the French toast.

"Oh! When I was at Zabar's, I ran into Melissa. Next week she wants to have us over with Leslie and Kurt."

Amber's father nodded, "Wonderful."

"Sorry, Amber, sweetie, you'll be out of town. But they wanna hear all your recommendations. They're planning a Europe trip for December and might stop in Italy."

"Sounds good," Amber endowed to her father the plate of French toast, which had been to celebrate her imminent departure.

"Honey. It's brioche. Brioche French toast. I got the bread from Zabar's." Amber's mom emphasized.

"I'm sorry, mom. I just—" She had stopped enjoying the taste of syrup years ago.

"Not even a bite?" Amber's father asked, though he didn't wait for her answer. He plopped the last bite into his gaping mouth, licked his lips, bit down, scraping the gooey remnants from his face with his teeth. He picked the dish up and licked the syrup and now-melted whipped cream and butter from the crevices left unscraped up by his fork.

Amber's stomach churned. She felt the wetness inside her mouth increase and believed it was anxiousness tyrannically overtaking her body. But no, her queasiness originated from the eggs. Perhaps it had been that especially clear and jiggly bit of the scramble—the one that felt veiny to the touch of her fork. Whatever it was, however, was coming back up her throat.

She ran to the bathroom and squatted on the floor in front of the toilet seat. She hadn't thrown up in years. The acid, fat, salt and sweet feeling of esophageal pain. Wheezing and gagging till she rid herself of the contaminant.

Her diaphragm squeezed. Her glottis stopped air, her pyloric sphincter slammed shut, and her abs contracted so much it felt like a barre class. A yellowish-brown gelatinous goo filled the bowl. Amber heaved, energy depleted, but task completed. Maybe the French toast would have kept the egg down.

She wheeled her suitcase from her bedroom, grabbed her filled-to-capacity dusty-dark-blue Fjallraven backpack, and double-checked that she had her international adapter, phone, charging cord—

"Do you have your passport?"

"Yes, Dad. I have my passport." Her voice was too hoarse. She wondered if they heard her throwing up before. Had the plaster walls hidden her heaves? She never wanted to eat eggs again.

"Do you have sunscreen? You're like your father, so pale. You'll bake out there in the sun."

"Mom, I have so much sunscreen packed. TSA is gonna think I'm deranged."

"Just want to make sure my baby doesn't burn up."

"Make sure you send us the contact information of the people you're staying with. Just in case. What's the place called again?"

"Dad, I'll be fine. I've like—stalked them online. They seem great. They have, like, a son who's my age and, it's all gonna be great."

"But still. In case anything happens. Just so we have it."

"You didn't tell us they had a son."

Amber's phone buzzed. "I think my Uber's downstairs."

Kisses and hugs. Promises for future messages and FaceTime calls—

"And of pictures and updates!" Amber's mother insisted.

"Yeah, Mom, I know. It's not like I'm leaving forever. I'll be back before you know it."

More kisses and hugs and tears despite the fierce denial of their presence.

Jason The Uber Driver played *Bring Me to Life* by Evanescence the entire drive to the airport. Amber put in her earbuds and tried to focus on Ira Glass' sweet, sweet voice. Her mind turned off as she listened to that week's episode of *This American Life* while she watched the city drift away.

She felt her own aliveness in a way normally made unattainable by her usual mental compulsions. Her physical dissociation from the city's grounds allowed her space to wield that same concreteness.

The toll was paid. They reached the terminal. Jason opened the trunk and took out her suitcase. Amber thanked him and rated him five stars. She grabbed her passport from her backpack and walked inside to get her ticket and go through security. It was as painless as TSA can be. Babies cried. People were invasively searched. Water bottles were chucked in the trash. Bare feet hit the gross floor. Police dogs sniffed for bombs.

At the gate, Amber bought a medium-sized coffee that tasted too burnt and too watery, which made for the perfect cup of airport coffee. It was too milky and watery, yet still acidic enough to further scald her mouth, eat away at her teeth's enamel, and even turn her stomach.

She could have purchased a breakfast sandwich or a muffin, or even had one of the snacks she packed to re-nutrify and quell her body's post-vom ache. She didn't. She liked the physical self-awareness brought about by her discomfort.

She opened her copy of *If on a Winter's Night a Traveler* by Italo Calvio, but failed to do as the book instructed and read. Instead, she listened in on the nearby chatter about the mediocre Entenmann's lemon poundcake acquired at Hudson News, which tasted of childhood. And hadn't Entenmann's stopped manufacturing Twinkies? But Twinkies were for sale at the Hudson News. And there was this one lemon poundcake they had once in Provincetown. Melted in your mouth, but was gooey and crumbly. It had poppyseeds in it, so maybe that influenced the chemistry of it all. They wondered when the opiate part of poppies gets activated. Isn't it strange how poppy seeds can make things so darn delicious? Maybe too delicious. One of them knew a guy who failed a drug test because they ate everything bagels every day for breakfast. The others did not believe this.

The coffee hadn't been a good idea. Her body was rebelling. If there had been anything but bean water in her belly, she'd surely be bent over in the bathroom upchucking its contents. She clung on to the fluids, tightening her abs like Jane Fonda.

She felt like this meme Emma had sent her the last time they went out clubbing together, when Emma was trying to take Amber's mind off everything—it said "drunk me telling drunk me not to throw up" overlaid over a photo of Beyoncé's projection looking down at Beyoncé herself.

Remembering that night meant remembering the forced forgetting. Fuck.

Amber was in the last boarding group, so she just stood from the side and watched as people edged their way closer to try and get on the plane seconds before someone else. They collectively craved to lay claim to their rented space.

The person in the window seat was passed out by the time she sat down. Thankfully, Amber had the aisle seat. She hated when she had to ask someone to move so she could get up, move around, go to the bathroom. Plus, the politics of how many bathroom breaks is normal and acceptable depending upon the length of the flight. Wondering how badly her seatmate was judging her bladder. Not being able to spread her legs out wider, like she could in the aisle seat—even if only another inch or so. Her feet had an unfortunate habit of falling asleep. Any extra space allowed her more room to shake them awake.

She missed the view, but flights were for sleep, when possible. It was better not to have temptation. She could barely stand to digest a sentence of words on a page as it were. She shifted in her seat. Scrolled through the entertainment offerings. Shoved her backpack further down under the seat in front of her.

Amber stared at Calvino's words as she listened to the safety presentation, flipping through its pages passively her eyes briefly lingered on the line reading, "if a book truly interests me, I cannot follow it for more than a few lines before—." She tucked the book in the magazine holder, then looked at the food and beverage menu. She decided that she would probably opt for the vegetarian option when they came around and asked about food. Hopefully they would have that Tilman's cheese plate? With the grapes and crackers and pre-cut apple slices, Ghirardelli over 70% dark chocolate, an assortment of nuts. And a drink along with the cheese plate. Though she could get behind a shitty pasta dish. She would enjoy pretty much anything composed of carbs that felt slightly overcooked and tough when chewed. A few pieces of vegetal mass thrown into the mix to help wet her mouth and aid with swallowing.

Something about the pre-packaged nature of airplane food, the way it was reheated and prepared and regulated. Amber loved eating everything she was handed, knowing it had been portioned and tested. She never really ate bread at restaurants. But on planes, of course she ate the bread. The main meal, bread, snacks, dessert, and drink options had all been chosen specifically to suit her needs as a traveler. This meal had been planned for her and all the other travelers seeking sustenance. Airline capitalists had labored over the menu for their benefit. Enjoying this meal was praxis.

Perhaps with the meal she would request sparkling water—she always called it sparkling water on flights, even though she just meant seltzer, which was actually just the name of some random town in Germany that made bank off their naturally fizzy water. She would ask for sparkling water, not seltzer—though she wouldn't specify "not seltzer," as she just had to herself, as that would be false, since the two things were synonymous—and a glass of red. That would really turn her stomach. Coffee with creamer, red wine, and bubbles—she'd have to eat the food before drinking the wine.

One of the benefits of international air travel was the free booze, and the assumed of-age-hood. Though asking for wine during the first round of the drink cart circuit felt thirsty and would make Amber look like a child and an alcoholic. Not cute. If she waited till dinner, however, it would seem a fun and sensible, spur-of-the-moment decision, Amber decided.

She fell asleep before the food came around. It was better this way, sleeping through most of the flight. But when she awoke, her stomach ached for caloric relief. She willed herself to sleep again. And then they were landing in thirty minutes. And she stayed awake and put away the Calvino, back in her backpack, not pretending to read it any longer. She looked out the window, over her seatmate's unconscious body. But she couldn't see anything, only blankness.

Take Your Medication, Roman

Take a short vacation, Roman, you'll be okay

—Nicki Minaj

It was still dark outside, but hot and humid. Amber's body dampened upon entry into the outdoors. She scooted into a cab, and in apologetic English, asked the driver to drop her off at any hotel. Her shoulders rose to her ears.

"What's the name? Of the hotel."

"No, sorry, I can find one online, but any hotel works. If you know any—sorry, my phone's dying." She felt bad for being so grossly American.

"A hostel or a hotel?"

"A hotel, I think? Just anyplace, doesn't matter, just any hotel."

The cab driver nodded. He drove and she watched the city reveal itself scene by scene, like some great movie. He dropped her at the Villa Borghese Rooms and urged her to waste away her day at the park.

She thanked him, and got out of his car. He helped her with her luggage. The air was heavy and she was dewy. She wondered if the air would be this thick and sticky in Trevinano. She pulled out her phone, then remembered it was low. 11%. Fuck. She needed an outlet. The cab driver wished her well and asked if he should wait for her to make sure the hotel would suffice.

She said she'd be fine. He bowed his head, and got back into the driver's seat.

Amber entered the building which was not as fancy as it looked from the outside, though the plaster walls were old and well-constructed in the way things no longer were.

She asked the concierge if they would hold her luggage in storage. The concierge said it was possible and handed her a plastic card with the number "38" written on it, in exchange for her belongings. She wondered if they were really storing luggage for 38 visitors or if they had just handed her that number at random.

She needed coffee.

She needed to text Alessandra. Where would they meet? Alessandra had said they would figure out where in the morning, but now it was the morning. Would it be too forward, texting first? Alessandra was handling business in the city, she had said, but Amber wondered what Marco and Luca were doing right then. If they felt as hot and sweaty as she did.

She wondered if she would visit them when she came back to Italy. Would they feel like family by the end? She wanted Alessandra to teach her how to make jam, though she supposed jam-making couldn't be that tricky. Her eyes felt heavy; she really needed coffee.

"Dov'è—caffé?" Amber barely squeaked out.

In skilled English the concierge suggested she try the Hard Rock Cafe, assuring her that the chain really brings the city to life, that even "Their ceilings are painted!"

"That's so cool! But, so I'm only here for a bit. In Rome. And I was just hoping—"

"I understand. But they have a great New York cheesecake with chocolate, toffee—."

"I'm actually from New York—."

"Your cheesecake is very good. Wow. I'm a fan."

"Yes, yeah, it's—I'm only here for a few more hours. Is there any place—?"

The concierge's gleaming eyes glazed over, bored again. He said, "Sorry. It's almost my lunch break. I don't know. Maybe Harry's Bar? It's famous, the bar. Fellini filmed there, *La Dolce Vita*." He looked around for confirmation, but they were alone in the lobby— air quiet, dust settled—but the concierge was correct. The bar had been featured in *La Dolce Vita*.

Amber said that sounded perfect and asked for directions as she internally chewed herself out for not having watched yet another one of Fellini's cinematic staples prior to her arrival.

Directions were exchanged for thanks. Amber grabbed a card with the hotel's information, and texted Alessandra its image on WhatsApp. Alessandra responded promptly with an audio message, which due to the mediocre quality of the recording, Amber was only mostly certain said something along the lines of, "How convenient I will be having a work appointment at Harry's Bar, which is close by. Why don't you meet me there around 4:30 or 5?"

Amber had to laugh. At least she'd know where she was going later on.

Amber walked out of the hotel as she responded to Alessandra saying that sounded good. That she would be there between 4:30 and 5. Alessandra responded within the minute with a voice message, "Great, closer in we will figure out the exact time we should meet. But sometime between 4:30 and 5 should be perfect. 4 at the earliest. No later than 5:30. Between 4:30 and 5 should be—great. How wonderful we are both in Rome."

Though Amber found it exceptionally strange that Alessandra continued to send audio recordings instead of texts, she found herself profoundly touched by the message itself. It was rather ridiculous that she should find herself in this foreign land meeting a family with whom she would temporarily live. It was all kind of sweet.

They could be serial killers. Amber could be a murderer. But they were all blindly placing their trust in each other. There was something so beautiful and hopeful about that. But what if they were boring? Annoying? Mean? What if they kidnapped her? Was that even possible? They couldn't *kidnap* her—she was going to live with them of her own free will. But what if they made her live there forever? No, no. What if they hated her? Despised her? Thought her insane? But if she was kidnapped—by Alessandra or her husband, or even her son. What if it was a family operation? Would she rebel? Growl at them, try to convince them she had gone crazy. She was acting crazy. What would it take for her to — like, would she be able to hold out hope that her parents and friends and the US government would come knocking on their door one day? Would she just end things quickly, slit her arm the long way with the razor they would afford her since she was a girl and should have no body hair. What if the Podere had no WiFi? That was ridiculous. All the emails and voice messages—.

She needed her mind to stop spiraling. She needed caffeine in her veins. And water. Her mouth felt dry. Was she dehydrated? She needed food. She needed to charge her phone. She couldn't think. Her stomach was aching, her feet were still tingly, half-asleep. Her mind was sleepier. She put her phone in her pocket and looked up. Remembered that she was in Rome. She giggled. She whispered so only she could hear—not that anyone else was around to listen—"Holy fuck."

The interior of Harry's Bar felt so grand and abandoned during the daytime in a way that almost made it seem cheap and phony. Without so much as opening the menu, Amber ordered herself a water, tiramisu, and a cappuccino. It was early enough in the day that the Italian waitstaff wouldn't judge her for drinking milk with espresso. And as for the tiramisu, her Elementary Italian 1 teacher had long ago taught her the word itself roughly translates to "pick-me-up," which seemed to be exactly what her body craved: the stimulating effects of sugar on the brain. Amber craved the days when her only highs were sugar. She remembered that she hadn't brought her meds, and her pulse quickened. She slowed her breath purposefully, to slow down her racing heart.

The movie theatre of her mind imagined the look of the ladyfingers soaking in coffee and sugar and eggs, mascarpone, and cocoa. Would it be large or delicate? The cream thick or too thin? Amber remembered reading some article about how tiramisu specifically works as an aphrodisiac and was served in brothels in Treviso, the city of its very invention. Didn't dessert always exude sex? Dinner was too marital, too much muchness, a longing for something more, something sweet and soft, rich. That was the issue: dinner was never satisfaction enough. Amber needed something sweet to satiate her hunger, and show her body it had finished its bout of consumption. She needed to finish, and also topped off with something fruity, decadent, rich and utterly unnecessary. Pointless for the nutrification vital to her existence. She would be the thirsty husband hooking up with the pool boy. And the babysitter. And his college girlfriend when she visited town.

Amber craved sugar. Something that made her heart—and not her body—burst. She held her stomach with her right hand. She was so tired she didn't care how insane she looked. She grasped her tank top, but really her own flesh. She felt her size. She wondered how many calories were contained in her own flesh. Was she like a chicken?? Did her skin take up more of her energy index than, say, her heart? She loved eating chicken skin, crisped with some rosemary and lemon-seasoned on top. She needed energy to enter her body. Her mind was guiding her thoughts in the oddest directions. She almost felt like she was dreaming, and the golden hue of the city of Roma was not doing much to prove wrong this unsaid conspiracy. She hated that she called Rome "Roma," even if to herself. She felt like a phony, adopting the easy Italian-isms. Soon enough, she'd be saying "grazie" instead of "thank you" without even hating herself just a little for it. That's what bugged her most. The plasticity and randomness of words and their selection. She had no real agency, just mere location and exposure. Thoughts were Mad Libs: she got to say what's scary and what's funny or pretty or sunny, but the whatever is still whatever with or without her.

Her cappuccino came, made thick with whole milk. She felt hollow inside, so the fluids felt comforting, like they were filling her stomach's lining with a warm embrace. Cocoa powder sprinkled abundantly on top. There were probably 230 calories in the whole cup. It was such a large cappuccino that she wondered if they had made her a latte instead. She wondered how much more milk goes into a latte versus a cappuccino. She knew there was more, but how much more? Regardless, she sipped her drink up in an instant, feeling her stomach fill. She remembered her phone. Shit. Down to 9%. A bunch of texts from her mom and dad, a few Instagram notifications: Like. Like. Like. Comment: ur pr3tty follow bck? Direct message. Like. Follow.

The waiter came over with her tiramisu. She asked him if there was an outlet she could use, luckily, she remembered to put her adapter in her carry-on. He nodded and offered to charge her phone inside. She handed it over, and felt a weight greater than 4.55oz abandon her. She smiled, then turned to examine the tiramisu: flat and wide, not tall and layered. She wanted more cream to squish in between her teeth. She imagined each morsel of sugar consumed gnawing away at her own enamel, filling her mouth's holes.

She picked up her fork, which felt heavy in her tired hand. Her stomach throbbed in anticipation. She strategically excavated her first bite from the rest, making sure to get the perfect cream-to-ladyfinger ratio onto her fork. She shut her eyes as she covered the fork with her mouth. She sucked its tines clean.

The cream evaporated into her saliva quickly, leaving the ladyfingers alone on her palate. She let it rest on her tongue and slowly applied pressure. She squished down the spongey biscuits and forced the alcohol residing in between the biscuit molecules to ooze out: sweat from pores.

The first time Amber remembered having tiramisu was with her mother while her grandmother was in town visiting from New Jersey, likely for a birthday or the holidays. Amber must've been about eight. They had gone to Cafe Lalo, her grandma's favorite New York establishment despite their food not being great and their staff being rude. The ambience was cute, and most importantly, it had appeared in the 1998 classic *You've Got Mail*. The movie predicted a generation for whom meeting significant others on the internet would be the norm, and Cafe Lalo is where the big first-IRL meet-up takes place.

But Amber remembered sitting with her mother and grandmother in the back corner of Cafe Lalo, tables away from where Meg Ryan sat. Amber ordered a hot chocolate, her mother a coffee, and her grandmother an amaretto. When it came to dessert, her grandma made the calls. An eclair, tiramisu, and a slice of carrot cake. The carrot cake was—

"Too dry and the icing is so sweet, but - why isn't it cream cheese? Carrot cake should have a—right?" Amber's grandma said.

Amber's mother nodded benignly, sipping her coffee, running her hands through Amber's hair as she said, "Try the tiramisu."

"Well, I have to try the eclair first," she took a bite of the eclair and said, "Oh it's—the pastry's too, fluffy."

"I like the tiramisu, Ma, try it." Amber's mother said to her mother.

She finally took a bite. "It's a tiramisu. I don't know what there is to like about it or not like about it. It's a—it tastes like tiramisu."

"Isn't that what you want when you order tiramisu?" Amber's mother asked. Amber smiled wide and looked up at her mother, which in retrospect, was likely an inappropriate showing of her taking sides.

"In theory, yes, but I'd rather someone revolutionize the dish for me. I don't need another tiramisu. I've had so many tiramisus before—"

Amber's mother pursed her lips and said, "What'd I do now?"

"Nothing."

"Clearly, I did something. How did I mess up?"

"I'm just trying to think what the plural form of tiramisu would be. I think maybe you'd just say I've had tiramisu so many times, because I can't—I don't know how—"

"Oh, for godssakes. Why are you worrying yourself with-"

"I'm sorry."

"My point was just that I've had tiramisu before. I don't need just another tiramisu."

"I've never had tiramisu before." Amber said. Her mother and her grandmother turned to face her. They seemed to have forgotten she was present and had the capability to think.

"Have a bite, hun," her mother said.

Amber picked up her fork and leaned her body over the table to select the perfect bite.

"Save some for us." Her grandma joked. Amber's mother released a loud and breathy exhale. But it had been a big bite, so Amber nibbled at it, nursing it. She ate her first forkful in multiple bites. Cradling her fork and nibbling on the food is held for her.

"What do you think?" asked her mother.

Amber doesn't remember what she thought of it. She wasn't actually sure if any of this was what was said or if this conversation actually happened. She could very well have conflated moments and memories and Frankenstein-ed the story in her head.

But even if none of it really happened, it was all true. When Amber thought of tiramisu, this is the story that felt like the beginning of her relation to it. And when she bit into the tiramisu at Harry's she couldn't help but feel like she was in a romcom, even though she wasn't not being semi-stood-up by her internet date. She was just a girl. Sitting alone in a restaurant in Rome. Eating a tiramisu all on her own. With a stomach that felt slowly sickened by this sweet.

Chilled mascarpone and was that cinnamon? Mixed in with the coffee and powdered cocoa. Saccharin particles broken down by the enzymes turning the starch to maltose and dextrin, commencing digestion before the bite hit her throat or stomach lining. She swallowed and felt the cream and carbohydrates continue to deflate as her body fluids attacked this alien invader, which filled her body with empty calories. She felt sick. She tasted egg. Was there egg in tiramisu? There had to be. Egg whites, at the very least.

She should have taken a photo of the tiramisu when she still had her phone. But she really should have texted her parents right after she landed, saying she had arrived safely and without a hitch.

She hoped they weren't worried, but of course they would be. She knew they'd pretend they were chill about her forgetting to text. Like, they wouldn't be angry with her or anything like that. They wouldn't be too worried. Just worried enough. As present parents ought to be.

She wouldn't try and squeeze in a quick trip to the Vatican. She wasn't going to let herself get caught up with all the things she was supposed to do and see. The "when in Rome!" mentality.

For example, she hated Aperol Spritzes. She wasn't going to have one. They were always too sweet. She far preferred Campari. Not even a Campari Spritz. Campari *soda,* which cut out the sweetening agent: Prosecco. And she hated day-drinking anyway. It always made her want to nap.

She would listen to the cab driver's advice and go to the park once she finished eating and charging her phone. She wouldn't concern herself with seeing everything else, or even anything else.

God, her stomach was really feeling queasy. Perhaps she should have gotten a sandwich. Or something with bread. Scrambled eggs mixed in a bowl. Coffee poured on top. Sugar-sprinkled. Cream-doled. Ladyfingers dropped on top. Scrambled eggs undercooked. But scrambled into the dessert. Beat into a fluffy cloud, but raw on the inside. Uncooked, unready for consumption. Ready to spoil her. Her meal had been spoiled.

She had never been able to make herself throw up. She had aspired to be a successful bulimic growing up. In a way, you got to eat your meal twice. Once going in and then again going out.

In second grade, she became obsessed with how penguin mothers chewed the food for their offspring and regurgitated it into their mouths.

Amber tried one time to chew food for her mother, but instead of accepting a French-onion-soup-filled kiss, her mother yelled at her and said, "Amber, honey, you don't—that's disgusting. You can't play with your food like that! Kids are starving and you're trying to, feed me? Like I'm your penguin child? Why couldn't you study the tufted titmouse or a woodpecker?"

"Woodpeckers are notorious for being mean," while penguins were bulimics for a cause. And that was beautiful. They ate food; let it rest in their stomach acids for a few hours. Then throw up so their loved ones could survive.

But just as Amber began to fetishize bulimia, she started doing some Googling and read that it could lead to heart palpitations, a damaged or burst one's esophagus, stomach rupture, intestinal perforation, diabetes, or even malnutrition. She knew she could never be successfully bulimic, since she'd be too afraid of the health risks. But still, when her second-grade teacher asked her what she wanted to be when she grew up, she said, "A mother penguin." Her teacher thought that was adorable.

Her body fluids disappeared the tiramisu; Coca-Cola eats the paint.

Amber worried she'd made a mistake ordering the tiramisu. It had seemed so spontaneous and fun in the moment, but, on an empty stomach?

She hadn't had sugar for breakfast since January, when she had inhaled left-over flourless chocolate cake for sustenance the first morning of the year. She had passed out by 1pm that day, but that may have been because she had not gone to sleep the night prior. It had been New Year's, after all. She spent it with Emma and Charlie and Laney and Robby. But Emma ditched early to go chill with her girlfriend, so by the time they made the saccharine decision, it had been just Amber and the "axis of depravity," as that cursed trio liked to call themselves.

But she had been dealing with intense insomnia, so perhaps anything that eventually led to rest was good? Sometimes it took a stupid hiccup in routine to propel her body into a state of slumber. She was obsessive enough to relish rituals, but easily bored enough to crave disruption just as regularly. Hence her escape to this Italian land.

She forced herself to swallow her last bite of overpriced cream and chocolate dust. She licked her lips and took a sip of water to clear her throat. She scanned for her waiter so she could ask for the check. She wanted to pay and leave so quickly, mainly so she could retrieve her phone and not seem like a hassle. She hoped it had enough charge to get her to wherever she was going. She would use it frugally, the phone. She wouldn't check to see what had happened in the past short while on the internet. She didn't need to know if anyone had posted in the past however many minutes. She didn't need the validation of e-companionship. No, she would go to the park across the street, and she didn't need directions for that.

The waiter turned a corner, edging into view. She was able to flag him down and get the check and her phone back. She paid. Took a trip to the bathroom.

She had consumed so much sugar and caffeine. She felt a burp rise up inside her. She went into a bathroom stall but didn't sit down. She just stood there and faced the toilet seat.

She unlocked the door to leave, but then changed her mind. She re-locked the door. Sat down. Then squatted in front of the toilet as her body retched. Tears glazed her eyes. Her mouth tasted sweet. Her teeth felt weak.

At first the liquid came out in small bursts. But by the third retch, the milky-coffee-tasting vomit splattered across the entire toilet. She dry-heaved a lot before she could calm down her breath and ease her heart. She ripped off some toilet paper and carefully cleaned the toilet bowl. She wondered if the walls were so thin the waitstaff could hear her. Did they know she was throwing up right now? Did they think she was bulimic? This wasn't bulimia. This was—she wasn't sure what this was. She hadn't thrown up in forever, and now—perhaps she was getting sick? What would this be? She had never had food poisoning before, but perhaps this was that. Her body was so good at rejecting what it required.

She washed her hands thoroughly and splashed water on her face, wiping the food remnants from her neck and chin and cheek. She tried to blink the glassiness from her eyes. She didn't want to look like she had just been sick. Like she was sick.

The gelato and coffee-sellers who lined the park smiled at her but mostly minded their own business, which she appreciated as the mere thought of more coffee or more sugar only further highlighted the rawness of her throat and the taste of regurgitated food that was once inside her.

What had made her sick? Her last supper in New York??

The acids gnawing away at her stomach lining left her wondering if she should eat the Kind bar she had packed. The fear of further upsetting her stomach mixed with her desire for a more comforting form of sustenance, like pasta or rice, led her to stewing over possibilities for future consumption.

She wondered how long it took a body to rely upon its own fat stores for fueling. If she'd reach that point before dinner. If she'd ever let herself get there. She had a knack for gaining invisible weight. Pounds that blended into her flesh, and begat additional body mass. Had she willed upon herself this bout of food poisoning?

Lots of big, graceful, sporty dogs were out with their owners. Some people were running or working out. Some were even on lunchtime romantic strolls. She continued down the path, and wound-up smack in front of the Borghese Gallery.

There was a ticket available for purchase, which the ticket-seller assured her was, "Most strange, very lucky. We really generally recommend you purchase tickets ahead of time as we do sell out regularly."

Amber nodded, but wasn't sure what good that knowledge would do her. Who knew if she'd ever come to Rome again, let alone this museum? She wanted to return to Rome. See more of it. But only in that passive way. The way that everyone wants to go to Melbourne and Dubai, Hamburg and Bucharest. She wanted to make the present feel like living out nostalgia—never to think it would be her last or only time someplace. It was better to imagine *the whens* and *in the futures* that would never come to be *nows*. YOLO praxis! But not in a cursed 12-year-old way that involves getting sick from fruit roll-ups and carnival rides—YOLO praxis in the way that Amber used death as a coping mechanism, which forced her to breathe and go on. Death was her comfort. When panicked, as she slowed her breathing and felt her pulse, she would whisper sweet reminders of her inevitable destruction. How these worries were pointless, as her life itself was pointless. She knew this sounded depressing, but to her, this was solace.

But maybe she should visit the Vatican after all. What if she never did make it back to Rome? Amber wasn't religious, but what if she was wrong? If there were a God—if God existed??? Would God be mad that Amber didn't visit the Vatican? She presumed they/she/he/we/xe/it/God? would be angrier with her over not believing in, well, God. Would visiting the Vatican lessen the punishment for her unbelief? Would God simply chastise her, tell her she'd been naughty, or would there be actual punishment? Was God cruel, or kinky? How bad a girl had Amber been, God? Did Amber have a

God complex? But not like she thought she was God or anything, just in the ultimate daddy issues sort of way.

Jesus Christ.

She closed her eyes and pictured Him. Why was his hair in a man bun? The man she pictured up on the cross wasn't Jesus-Jesus. Obviously. But he wasn't even her conception of Jesus? Was that - the barista from her local Joe's? She couldn't shake the image of her barista-as-Jesus from her mind, but she imagined the God-punishing-Jesus-to-absolve-all-Christians-thing and God hammering a nail into barista-Jesus' hand, and making her watch—and in a way, she was making *herself* watch? Maybe she did have a God complex. But no, God was the ultimate voyeur and made a world full of sinners in his own image. Or maybe there was no God, and Amber was just a voyeur with an external locus of control, placing her sadistic fantasy of giving Jesus what he wants: pain.

There had to be a religious subsection of PornHub. She pulled out her phone and opened up Notes. She wrote down a note reminding her to look up "religion." Though she supposed that search could go in a different direction than what she had meant. Maybe she'd have to look up "God roleplay" instead. She realized she hadn't been turned on in a while. How she'd kind of turned that part of herself off. But she wasn't going to let her think about any of that here.

Here was for thinking about things that were not that. She wasn't going to let Charlie win and invade her mind even on vacation. Too bad all she wanted was a vacation from her own mind. Maybe that would be impossible.

The museum guards finally started letting in the ticket-holders for the 1PM time-slot. They filed into the sterile, white hallway like a trail of young school kids.

Amber craned her neck up to look at the ceiling, which was saturated with cotton candy colors and painted pretend statues holding up art, surrounded by painted people prepared for battle, riding clouds and horses.

She rolled her head around, back to its regular orientation. People filed around her, quickly buzzing by, rushing toward whichever piece called to them with a silent siren call. She smiled in the way that's embarrassing, almost gloating.

She floated from room to room, trying to breathe in the essence of all the profound beauty. Breathing in the paint particles, the old air recycled by means of new bodies and life. Air she ate with her mouth stretched wide, that smelled like artificial museum air.

She would live and die on the substance. It was addictive. She suffocated herself with the Borghese air. She needed more but taunted herself with less. Her fast, shallow breaths made her think of urgent care. Panic. Fainting.

She could faint right there in the gallery. She was so overwhelmed. Not by the people present, but by the people of the past who made this.

The idea of orange juice popped into her head. The thought of pulp led to sweet salivation. Perhaps it was the fainting-feeling that reminded her of her recent reviver. She always drank orange juice to help her blood sugar. Not that her blood sugar needed help. Not that her blood pressure needed help, either. Amber confused blood sugar and pressure too often to be a good hypochondriac.

She was worried about her current state: sick on nothing. Insatiable and unfeedable. She knew she shouldn't WebMD it, but made a mental note to search it anyway. Because of course she was going to freak herself out about it. Likely for no reason.

But right then it was the art, not her panic or even the weather, that made her sweat. She had never wanted to lick a statue before. Or finger-fuck a cut painting. Or shop the collection of ceramic crucifixes like they were dildos waiting for erotic insertion. Amber edged closer to the lined-up crucifixes, seeking their Creator: Lucio Fontana. She spun around and stalked close to a copper-colored slab with one slice down its center, and found confirmation: Lucio Fontana.

She was Noah on the Ark as dopamine flooded her brain.

The Berninis were great, but the Fontanas tore open her heart like a jagged piece of broken glass. She didn't know how he did it: make space and add dimension through destruction.   He harmed his own art. He marked up and negated them. He punctured the skin of the piece and created spacious unspace in the broken plane of the Art. She imagined Lucio taking an X-ACTO knife, or better yet a boning knife or a butcher's knife or a cleaver, and carefully cutting his image from top to bottom. But when she imagined him doing it, she imagined him doing it to her vulva. From vagina to anus: hole to hole. She didn't know how Fontana's negation of his art's wholeness through hole-ness made her feel so— holy? And whole. She needed to pray. To whom? She had no clue. She needed to thank someone. Perhaps her cab driver.

Her eyes were burning by the time she found herself in the Caravaggio room. The pooled and pent-up tears streamed down her face, relenting. She was so embarrassed. She couldn't stop staring at *David with the Head of Goliath*. The phallic sword having swung and cut off the head, which looked to be in some sort of pained ecstasy.

She moved on to *St. Jerome*.

Whose skull was that? And what were the books? A cream color had never before shone brightly. She wished she knew the first lick about art; she couldn't bear to imagine how she would be feeling right now if she knew anything at all, for she knew nothing and she was already feeling everything. She couldn't imagine feeling anything more; if she felt anything more, she might have to die right there, which would honestly be a pretty iconic death. Take a breath, she told herself. But she wanted to scream and dance and hug everyone. She smiled at one of the security guards and tried to ask with her eyes, "Does it ever get old??? Are you as shocked at this beauty? Are you horrified? Have you ever felt more complete?"

She didn't even care she wasn't permitted to take any photos. She knew her blurry portrait-mode phone photos would only mar her remembrance. She couldn't capture this. No one would understand the suffocating effects of ecstatic art unless they experienced it for themselves. She felt like a tween, whining to her parents about a newfound fear of crushing isolation. But instead of feeling alone and scared, Amber felt like a time-traveler, finally learning that people have always felt the way she felt.

She stopped in the bathroom to relieve her bladder and gather herself by the mirror. How quickly bathrooms had transformed from serving as a necessary locale for a bladder reprieve into this purgatorial space for uncontrolled offerings.

While she washed her hands, she muttered little nothings trying to reorient and re-personalize. Stop dissociating. Dizzy with clarity, she allowed herself to use up a percentage point of charge to check the time.

It was ten past three. She figured she ought to get back to the hotel, maybe grab an espresso and charge her phone a bit. Let it juice up enough so she would not feel guilty responding to her parents' well wishes, and to Emma's twelve messages.

But by the time she retrieved her bag from the concierge, Alessandra had sent another audio message letting Amber know she was running early.

Amber returned to Harry's Bar. Her body liked knowing this one route. She pretended to know Rome, ending her time in the city having gone full circle.

She texted Alessandra:

I'm here !!! ready whenever u are !
but no rush !

And then her mother:

Spent the AM at the Borghese
about to meet Alessandra !!!
Really warm here but so pretty
Love you coco
*xox

Nothing ever seemed to happen in the summertime, and yet lives could be lived in minutes. Nothing was ever actually, irreconcilably different come September. And yet so many lively tales were birthed and aborted in the meantime. She wondered if Alessandra looked like her Facebook posts. She had tried to busy herself so she wouldn't keep speculating the hypothetical realities of this family she should soon come to know.

She Googled Lucio Fontana and found an article on the Tate's website on Fontana's *Spatial Concept, Waiting* and his *Tagli* (cuts). On the backs of his earliest works in this series, he wrote the word "attesa" if there was one cut and "attese" if there were multiple cuts, which according to the Tate's website translated roughly to "expectation" or—

"Amber?"

Amber looked up, feeling caught. "Hi!"

"This is all your luggage?"

Amber nodded.

Alessandra wore a baby blue, button-down blouse despite the heat. She had thick curly hair, a warm smile, and greenish-brown eyes. Her jeans were too big for her body. She was thick and radiated ease. "Let's get to the car, it's a few blocks away, but see the sky?" Amber hadn't looked upward since the Borghese. The clouds fogged the air and blocked the blue background from sight. The view of above was bright and white but lacking direct light. "It could start pouring any second now. This is why it's so stressful. You don't know if it will rain, if it won't rain. If it doesn't, the vines die. If it does, sometimes it hails the size of tennis balls and—well. You know, that's not so good. They die. We have a baby vineyard, and, there's no water. So, this is good, the rain, but—when did you get in to Rome?"

Amber tried to sanely explain her past few hours. They eventually reached the minivan. Amber sat shotgun and Alessandra drove. Amber was sort of surprised when the driver's seat was on the same side as it is in America. She wasn't sure why exactly she presumed it wouldn't be. Was England the only place in which they drove on the other side? She couldn't remember.

"What brought you to Rome?"

"Oh. A concert. And some business. We have to go to meet with buyers. We're still small, our vineyard. It's still new. We need them to, you know, buy it. The wine."

"What concert was it?"

"Oh yes, Yann Tiersen was performing. My friend goes to all the concerts. Has, um, seasonal tickets? So, she invited me to go with her. It was very fun. Are you familiar with the music?"

Amber's eyebrows met in consideration, "I've heard the name before—."

"I'll play you some," Alessandra fiddled with the dashboard and put his music on shuffle. "You must be tired, what with everything you've done. We have to stop by the store in Perugia before we get home, there are some things I need for dinner. Do you have any allergies? Anything you like to eat for breakfast?"

"Oh, whatever's fine. I'm easy."

"Bread and jam will be okay? For breakfast?"

"That sounds—yeah, great." Amber's stomach gurgled.

"Good. Are you sleepy? Nap, get rest. I'll wake you when we're at the store. Honestly, I'm tired from the concert, too. It's been go, go, go, go, *goooo*. You know?"

Amber laughed and said yeah, she did know. She counted cars until her eyelids gave up.

Ipercoop was a grocery store like any other grocery store, but Amber liked grocery stores. She loved the smell of bread and the coolness of the freezer aisles. The slight deviations and variations on mass-produced products' sameness. She particularly loved feeling like a child in a grocery store. Finding cheap nothings that fueled her brain with dopamine hits. She was an addict. She liked to make her mind happy with cereal boxes and candy wrappers—these bandaids helped the malady of life. Getting to follow the leader and do none of the labor of product-selection or purchasing. It was all Monopoly money while she walked through the artificial, fluorescent-lit maze filled with corn and crackers and tuna fish.

She especially liked grocery stores in foreign countries. Slight variation with much more sameness than not. This store seemed to be housed beside others, in a mini mall of sorts. It had oddly high ceilings for a supermarket. Maybe high ceilings were an Italian thing. Though she hadn't noticed that anywhere else. Everywhere should have high ceilings. Could they be that much more work? That much more expensive?? Height had never been something Amber spent much time thinking about; width had always been her main concern. But she tended to like being indoors more than she liked being outdoors, and high ceilings made being indoors even more bearable.

Amber decided Ipercoop was an iper version of Coop, a super coop—so just an offshoot? Alessandra grabbed some Coop-branded almond milk, butter, crostini, and bread.

"You're from New York, you said?"

"Uhuh. Manhattan."

Two bunches of carrots, three onions, four potatoes, and five zucchinis: two of which were pea-green-colored, one, bright and golden, and the final two, striped green-and-yellow.

Her stomach felt hollow—so hungry she didn't even feel hungry anymore. When hen he she he ate at next her stomach would ache. This his is premonition of her future pain made mad ma her want wan an to test her limits limit, her own ow mortality. She had never ever eve tried just—not no eating? Did id she he need food, really? Of course, that's what people are told: the information they feed students in school is that they do need food and water to survive but what if—wow, okay, Amber was really getting delirious and lightheaded; her thoughts were spiraling. Yes, she did require food. In fact, she feared she really needed to consume something soon to regain her sanity.

"We had someone else from New York come help us, but we didn't know—. He didn't like the country. Not—Italia, ma non si piace— he didn't like, uh, the dirt. The spiders. He thought it was—it was when *Call Me by Your Name* came out? Around then. He thought he would be sitting by the pool all day and eating pasta, you know? But we don't have a pool. It's work. Yes?"

"Yeah, no, I'm—I'm here to—I'm here to help."

Four knobs of ginger, five lemons, and three bananas—bruising and bright yellow. "This is how you want them. More nutrients when they're ripe," Alessandra said.

Amber remembered watching some video about this Chinese etiquette school that cost sixteen thousand dollars where they taught their pupils how to eat a banana elegantly: incisions and cuts, contents forked into mouths.

Mutti salsa pronto classica. Warmed, she imagined, it would smell of garlic. Mixed in with penne or tagliatelle.

"After two days I think he—he was wearing these clothes, not for work. For photos. After two days he said his grandma was sick and that he had to go home, which—life happens, but we depend on workers, you know? We only have so many rooms; we had to say no to others. And he just left."

Santa Rosa limoni marmellata. Imagine: on bread, gently toasted, maybe even accompanied by a soft cheese, like brie or camembert. Maybe even baked cheese, half-fluidified; losing its molded form. Smeared onto the bread like butter. But a butter so thick it got caught in the throat. A suffocating butter. A heart attack.

Amber wondered what Emma was up to right now. She felt bad for taking so long to respond to her messages, and for generally being a shitty friend as of late.

Alessandra said, "Crazy, yes?"

"Wow that's—I'm sorry."

"It's—life happens. You figure it out. I'm just—tell me if there's any food in particular you want, you know?"

"This all looks great. Thank you for—yeah, for feeding me."

"It's a trade, exchange, you know? You work, we—." she loosely gestured toward nothing, as if that explained everything. "Marco and I, we try to think—since most of the people who come are young, you know? We try to imagine if Luca went somewhere? How he would—how we would want people to treat him?"

Lavazza caffé and crema, and a package of Baci chocolates. Breaking into one of the chocolate circles, past its hardened shell and into its luscious center—.

"That's really lovely."

"And I do like to cook and we only eat healthy, organic things. You know? Good food." Alessandra waited a breath before saying, "You will like the work, I think."

"Amazing. Yeah?"

"It's very relaxing. Very rewarding. The manual labor. I think the city kids these days, you know, you have all this stress. You'll mostly be combing the vines. Marco will show you. And maybe some, uh, you know—weeding. Marco will be with the men. They have to irrigate because there's no rain? But you won't do that, it's not—the boys will do that. Your work is—you'll be on the old vineyard, not with the baby vines. It's good work. Nice to clear the head, yes? It's nice to work to make something—what's the word"

Amber didn't know.

"Tangible. To feed nature."

"That's beautiful."

Prosciutto: a hunk, unsliced. She imagined biting down on the big hunk of meat with her teeth, like the animal she was. Like a carnivore. Using her front teeth to rip and tear some cured flesh from the rest, then chomping repetitively with her molars, to mush its toughness. She'd swallow.

"Well, Trevinano is—a very special place. It looks Tuscan but it's not. It's—it borders Lazio and Umbria, and also Tuscany. It's very—you'll see. And you'll meet Luca and Marco, oh the boys. They're good, good boys. And Natalia—a sweet, sweet girl. You actually—you could be sisters. She and Luca used to play as children—we lived in Berlin when Luca was little. Natalia's father studied with Marco. When we needed help. She said she'd help since we need all the help right now. Because the rain. Our baby vineyard needs more water. It's not getting enough, yes? So—it's difficult."

Amber nodded, not sure if there was anything she should contribute.

"This is our friend's," Alessandra said, holding up a bag of fresh pasta. "Silvia. She's great. She made this. Handmade, organic. Very healthy. You're not vegetarian, no?"

"Oh, no, I'm—I eat everything."

Alessandra grabbed, instead, some Barilla-brand penne and spaghetti. Amber could be at Zabar's right now. Well, maybe not Zabar's. But Whole Foods or Eataly, even Gristedes.

"Good. Our last farmhand was, and I didn't know how to—it makes it harder. You know? You have to make sure they're getting all the nutrients. I made so many lentils. But you have to eat protein with the carbs to get the whole protein. You know this?"

Amber didn't know this. She nodded, hoping that would suffice. Then added, "huh—interesting. Makes sense."

Alessandra said, "Yes. It's very important."

Thirty-two ounces of cod. The current state of the cod: raw. What Amber saw, however, was its future: covered in batter, plopped into a pan-filled with oil, fried to a crisp. Topped with blistered tomatoes, maybe some olives.

There's that saying that the gut is like an octopus, the second mind of the body, whatever. Amber had that. Her gut was ruling her body. It croaked.

Alessandra kindly grimaced, and assured Amber that they would eat soon enough. Even if soon enough could not come soon enough.

They checked out, and returned to the car, both carrying a few bags. Alessandra looked up at the sky and said, "See? Even still. It could rain now, or in an hour. It could drizzle or storm. We just don't know these things."

Amber nodded. And wracked her brain for reasonable banter. "Do you normally have someone staying and helping out?"

"We try to. It's nice. Good for everyone, you know. Nice to help out a young person who wants to learn. And we need help. So, we try to have them. But it's hard. It changes our schedule. Sometimes I don't eat lunch, but when we have—you have to keep a routine."

"What's the schedule again, exactly?"

"It can change. You just will have work that has to—when there's work, it has to get done, you know? It's—the land doesn't wait. Sometimes we work all day, for hours, and then take some days off. But most times breakfast is around seven-thirty. Work starts eight o'clock until around noon. I'll have lunch ready by one. You have some time during the afternoon, it's too hot to work then—work five till seven or six, depending. Dinner at seven-thirty in the nighttime. We all eat together in the kitchen. Today you won't have to do any work, you can just—get settled, meet everyone—."

Amber nodded and tried to picture the next morning, afternoon, evening, and inevitably, what this repetitious mundanity would mean for her coming weeks and months of mornings, afternoons, and evenings.

The music hadn't started playing automatically when the car started back up, so instead they listened to the sounds of cars zooming through the open windows. Exhale.

Off the highway and into the hills, turning and turning. Luscious greenery breathing with wind, moving in waves with the soundless, rhythmic music of nature. One last turn, and—

"This is it," Alessandra reached up to the rearview mirror and clicked a button. The wrought-iron gates slowly swung open, and their two dogs barked their welcome. Alessandra shouted back to them, "Basta, Harry! Basta!!" then continued, "They're so—Marlena sleeps most times, she's, when I'm gone, she—but Harry, he loves to run. He always comes back, we just worry, that someone will drive without—so we try to keep him from leaving, you know? So, we keep the gates shut, just remember this."

Amber said, "Absolutely, I'll make sure to shut the gates when I—."

Alessandra finished parking the car.

It wasn't raining, or even overcast here. It was cloudy in that way that reminded Amber of the brightness of the sun more so than the wetness of the sky. Perhaps it had drizzled while she slept. Amber moved her right pointer and middle fingers to her throat and felt for her pulse.

Alessandra unbuckled and opened her side door without pausing for breath or further ceremony.

"Life itself is the proper binge."

— Julia Child

Olive oil sizzled on a hot pan, as caramelized onions mixed with diced and seared eggplant, now oozing fleshy innards out, proliferating, and forming sauce. Alessandra checked on the pot of water, which had come to a boil. She poured in a bag of whole grain penne. Steam rose and shrouded Amber's view. Her gaze broke from the stovetop, toward the sound of sturdy footsteps approaching.

The man had shoulders rounding forward and relatively long, jet-black hair. Matter-of-factly, yet somehow still frazzled, he mumbled, "Buonasera" to the room. Upon seeing Alessandra with his own two eyeballs, he glowed.

"Caro!!" Alessandra said, "Amber, this is Marco. Marco, ricorda che è- saluta Amber."

"Scusi, scusi, scusame. Ciao, Amber," Marco said while he walked to the stovetop, where he peered over Alessandra's shoulder, sniffing her work.

"Ciao! Grazie per—having me?"

Marco opened drawers and cupboards, gathering materials to set the table.

"Oh, sorry. I can—help?" Amber asked.

Marco waved her off, "Please, please."

Alessandra sawed off a few pieces of bread from a fresh-baked loaf. She cut each piece in quarters and placed them gently in a small, wicker container. She handed over two quartered pieces to Amber.

Amber felt starved, "Thank you, this looks—" she took a fat bite. The crust was doughy and thick, but not crunchy. Its innards were dense and dry. The bread was a desert, drowned by her saliva.

Alessandra simpered and said, "He speaks mostly Italian, so you know, don't be offended if he isn't so—if he doesn't make good conversation. He understands you are not so comfortable with Italian and he is not so comfortable with English, so, it is fine. Luca and I are pretty good with it, and Natalia, who you'll—well, you'll meet both of them."

"When did you get to Italia?" Marco asked, making eye contact with Alessandra.

Amber tried to speak in the tongue of the land, and responded, "Questa mattina, che è—"

"You were in Rome, yes?" Marco said.

Mouth full, Amber nodded.

"You've been before, though, no?" Alessandra said.

Amber shook her head, no.

The eggplant-and-onion sauce was now thick and gave the room a rich aroma, which smelled, to her, like Italy.

"Wine?" Marco asked Amber, as he carried down wine glasses from the cupboard and distributed them around the table.

"Oh! I mean, like, I would—sure? If that's okay. I would love—."

Marco placed a glass by her placemat and grabbed an apricot from the bowl in the center of the table, which was aggressively large and filled only with apricots. Orange, stubby, scuffed-up, and often yellowish or even greenish. He bit into his chosen fruit, took off the first half with his front teeth, held onto the pit, then popped the rest of the fruit into his mouth. He disposed of the pit in the compost over in the corner of the room.

Alessandra noticed Amber's captivation and said, "Oh, yes. Have some, Amber. I've already made, what, five batches of apricot jam. We have that and the fig jam in the morning. There are still some pears, but we have so many apricots. Please eat them. It's better they are eaten. If not—they rot and what can we do? They have to be wasted, thrown away."

Amber felt the weight of her arm as she reached up and hoisted her body up just enough to reach the center of the kitchen island. She hovered her hand above the bowl and searched for just the right apricot. She didn't think she had ever eaten one fresh before—

only dried, from Whole Foods. She found one that was perfectly rounded, smooth, not yet puckered with age. Pinkish-red spots accumulated, freckling one portion of its skin. Amber moved her hand down deliberately, like the claw from those machine games the kids play in Denny's at midnight. Her prized fruit felt tough, firm. She turned it over, to complete her inspection. The freshly-flipped-over side was not yet marred by dirt and grime, though. It had been aged, but protected. Like baby's fat wrinkled by water, almost pruned. Worn from exposure.

Amber bit in, enveloping the dried-up part with her lips chapped from travel—cutting into the apricot's fuzzy skin with her incisors.

It was sweet and not juicy, almost like a not-chewy fruit jerky—or one of those fruit leather things that used to be hip—it still held moisture. Amber disconnected the other half from its pit, and popped it into her mouth. She let it sit on her tongue for a second before she chomped it to pulp. The apricot's mush lingered atop her tastebuds. She spread it thin, allowing her tongue to smush the mush on the roof of her mouth and the backs of her teeth to interrogate for tasting notes and variance. It was too dry and the texture was unsatisfying. She didn't think she liked apricots very much and had the overwhelming desire to spit. She swallowed.

Amber opened her eyes. She hadn't realized her eyes had been closed. She realized no one had spoken. It was so quiet. Did they want to be alone? Should she engage them in conversation? "So, how long have you been doing this? Like, running the vineyard?"

Alessandra relayed Amber's question to Marco, "Sta chiedendo da quanto tempo abbiamola vigna."

Amber felt guilty for not even trying to use Italian. That was why she was here, after all. *To learn Italian, right, Amber?* Her inner voice said.

Alessandra answered in English, "About five years ago now we moved here from Rome and started making wine."

"What made you want to get into—?"

"I lived at home," Marco said.

Alessandra jumped in, explaining, "I was a lawyer, and Marco stayed home and took care of Luca. But then Luca was young still, and I was tired, and we wanted a break from the city, really. It made sense. We love wine, Marco especially. And Trevinano has good soil, interesting soil. Not many winemakers here, so it's exciting."

"Literally groundbreaking," Amber said. Neither Alessandra nor Marco got her wordplay.

A skinny, cigarette-eating boy entered—brooding eyes, careless attire, windswept hair.

"Ah Luca, mio caro!" Alessandra said as she rushed over to greet him. He looked tired and disinterested.

"Ciao, mamma, pappa—." he said, quite bored. "Ho annusato la cena dalla mia stanza. Quando stiamo mangiando?"

Amber had already lost track of the conversation.

"Presto, sarai scortese, vedi che abbiamo un ospite?" Alessandra said, tightening her smile.

Luca said, "Un ospite?"

Marco cleared his throat, and said to Luca, "Salutala, sii gentile. Tua madre è appena arrivata da Roma, non devi farla impazzire."

She understood the feelings. She had eyes. She just couldn't understand the words.

"Ciao! Luca, vero?" Amber said, trying to establish she spoke a few Italian words.

"Pensavo non parlasse italiano?" Luca asked his mother.

Amber said of herself, "Non parlo molto—e non parlo bene."

"Ciao, scusa," Luca said.

"Alessandra dice che parli inglese?" Amber said.

Luca said, "Yeah." Thank God.

Amber moved her limbs to the compost. She threw her pit in the pile of ort atop posthumously rotting fruitskin. She rubbed her eye, which wanted to be rubbed even though it wasn't itchy, and found her way back to her stool.

Luca sat and grabbed the ceramic water pitcher which lay out on the countertop. He poured some for himself then said to Amber, "Water?"

Before she could respond, Marco said, "Versane un po' per tutti, Luca."

"Si, Luca, aiuta tuo padre a apparecchiare la tavola," Alessandra said.

"Tutto è pronto, cara cara, ti stiamo solo aspettando," Marco said.

Luca said, "E per Natalia! Stiamo aspettando anche Natalia."

"Non stiamo parlando bene dell'italiano, proviamo a parlare più inglese, sì?" Alessandra said.

Marco and Luca begrudgingly nodded. Amber played with her placemat. She wasn't sure if they wanted her to understand or if they preferred this spoken privacy.

"Are you in Uni?" Luca asked Amber, who had forgotten that she was a participant in this scene, and had temporarily allowed herself to relax into her role as voyeur.

"Oh, me?" Amber said.

"Yeah?" Luca said.

"Yeah, I go to Princeton," Amber said.

"What do you study?" Alessandra said.

"I'm an English major, so just—literature. Luca, are you in school?" Amber said.

"English literature?" Luca said.

"No, just—books from wherever," Amber said.

"But your field of study is named English?" Marco asked.

"Yeah. I guess comp-lit is a different department. Luca, are you in school?" Amber said.

He nodded. "For business."

"What kind of business?" Amber said.

"Maybe hotels?" Luca said.

The floorboards groaned. Everyone turned to face the doorway.

Natalia, with her nest of black, bed-tousled hair, swinging arms and thudding steps. Her gait was that of a petulant schoolchild, walking to the principal's office for drawing an unsavory picture of a professor. Her eyes were a piercing, slate grey. The eyes tween-aged Amber had so lusted to possess. The eyes of Athena and Annabeth. And those lashes, so delicate, but plentiful. A smattering of freckles.

A chick responding to its mother's call; Amber whispered "buonasera" in response to the symphony of "buonaseras."

"Ah Natalia, this is Amber. Remember, I mentioned before I left for Rome."

"Nice to meet you!" She couldn't look Natalia in the eyes without staring—but Natalia stared back into hers. She wondered what Natalia thought she would find, considering she felt she had "dead horse eyes," which was a description she thought she stole from *30 Rock,* though maybe she'd dreamt it all up. Amber pictured Pavlov as she swallowed.

Natalia was the one to break their Bo Burnham-style "prolonged eye contact," but she did so with a grin, and a flirtatious roll of her eyes, fluttering of her lashes in Luca's direction. She sauntered over to perch on a stool beside Luca. He grazed his arm down her back.

Marco poured wine from a pitcher of their pre-bottled house blend.

Amber wondered how he and Alessandra decided how much was reasonable to drink themselves. Did they formally ration themselves? Did they buy wine, also? They must. Did they simply trust their guts not to consume their whole crop? How did they decide when to stop? Did people ever make their own label of wine just for their own private consumption? Or was wine always made for sale?

Alessandra portioned out the pasta, giving the most to Luca and Marco, then to Natalia and Amber, explaining, "The men, they need to eat. You are girls, so—." Alessandra served herself the least. Amber wondered if all the pasta she would eat this summer would make her fatter, or if she was only consuming carbs, if she would whittle down into nothingness. If the lack of nutrients would deprive her flesh so much, she'd be ripped, like a wrestler. Was the vineyard work going to be intense, or practically fake? It could honestly go either way. Amber could envision herself digging and weeding and getting physical, or listening to music in nature while noshing on the grapes as she picked them from their vines. Or maybe she could help with bottling wine, and making graphics. Interesting. She could be their vineyard intern and not the farmhand.

Pasta mixed with sauce. Did they only eat whole-grain?

Amber ground her teeth against the ridged body of the penne. Smushing the tubular pasta into a flat sandwich. Her body ached. Her stomach begged for her to hurry up, but her teeth enjoyed the chewing sensation too much. The pasta was so perfectly cooked al dente. Cardboard-like and sticky. Meatless, but meaty. Umami-ish, delicious. The sauce coated her throat and tantalized her stomach acids. The first bite was a striptease; her body craved more action. She took another bite—swallowed before the pasta had been well chewed.

She remembered she was expected to participate in the conversation. "So, Natalia? Are you—a student?" Her stomach felt queasy. She stabbed three pieces of penne, hoping an influx of food inside her would quell her slight nausea.

Natalia was mid-sip of wine, she allowed herself to swallow, then responded, "I'm studying psychology and Humboldt."

"How um? Bold of you," Amber said accidentally.

"What'd you say?"

"She said how *um-BOLD* of you," Luca repeated.

Was she getting her period? She felt like she was cramping almost?

"Natalia's been here for three weeks now, Amber," Alessandra said.

"Oh, wow," Amber said, before asking Natalia, "How long are you here for exactly?"

Natalia responded, "till school starts back up, most likely."

"You like the work, yes? It's good to focus, do the manual labor? No?" Alessandra said.

"Yeah, I've listened to a lot of audiobooks. Can't complain," Natalia said.

Gases threatened escape; Amber tightened her abdominal wall, which only forced the fleeing formless matter further up her body, out of her chest and toward the base of her throat.

Alessandra raised her eyebrows. "I don't know how you focus on the vines while you listen to books."

"I'd go crazy in the fields for that many hours, with only my thoughts," Natalia said.

"You teenagers are, too—you need to slow down," said Alessandra.

Amber nodded and, with a plastered smile, silently released a miniature burp.

Luca said, "Mom, we're not teenagers."

"You know what I'm meaning," Alessandra said.

"When'd you get to Italy? You're American?" Natalia said.

"This morning, actually—. I—yeah. I'm American," Amber said.

"You know what I just am realizing? All of us are from cities," Alessandra said while she and Marco carried their plates to their seats.

"Cool," Luca said, unamused. He ate quickly and aggressively, stabbing his food and downing his wine to lubricate his esophagus. Amber was reminded of home: her mother's pancakes, and her father.

Marco cleared his throat. "Luca, puoi aiutarmi e Stefano con l'irrigazione domani?"

Luca nodded, leaned over and grabbed a paper towel, which he used to scrub off the sauce he wasn't able to catch with his fork from his bowl. He got up and composted the soggy towel of remains, and placed his dirty dish and utensils in the sink. "A che ora?"

Natalia looked over at Luca right as he turned back to face the table. That was the first time his eyes softened. He smiled.

"Sette e mezza. Va bene?" Marco said.

"Si, si, si—" He casually dragged his nails along Natalia's back, "I'm gonna go watch a movie."

"Mhh. Mhm," Natalia nodded and took another bite—mostly eggplant carried by a piece of penne. She planned her bites, plotted the combination of sauce-to-grain. She made this bite big and full, then guided it to dock in her mouth. Meticulously masticating until the food was an even meal, ready for swallowing. She never stained her lips or required a napkin; she was clean and perfect. Amber didn't know how she did it. Her own napkin looked like Lee Krasner's Combat. Oily and orange, crimson. Fleshy purple-y undertones. Movement and randomness, a thoughtful attack of color announcing itself. Accidentally perfect, thoughtless but particular. Amber used her napkin like her record, an archive of her meal. She wiped away the excess leftovers from her lips and cheeks and recalled the first time she dyed her lips and tongue accidentally, with pomegranate seeds.

Amber swallowed one al dente piece of penne—una penna, would it be? Probably not. Didn't una penna mean pen? She figured she should probably just think of it as "a piece of penne," and yet she was set on pretending penna was the proper word, anyway. She took a swig of wine as her mouth muscles tensed against her palate; the nutritious materials were pushed by the tongue, which wriggled up and back against the hard palate, preparing her body to swallow, catapulting the food into her pharynx. From there the penna slid deftly to her esophagus. Amber swallowed too much air and had to belch, but couldn't bear to, which only made the belch more belchy. Natalia smiled, and encouraged a belch of her own. Alessandra's lips tightened; she was no fan of these air expulsions.

"This is lovely!" Amber said, red from embarrassment but not yet the wine. She took another sip.

Marco nodded, "Bene, bene."

"Trevinano wine has a very distinctive taste. We love it," Alessandra said.

Natalia swirled and sipped from her glass. She looked at Amber while she swallowed. Natalia looked like a black cat. Her arching back, bad posture—but elegantly bad posture. She caved in on herself, enticingly. Her hair was slick, and long, and overwhelming.

Something about her felt like anxiety—the good bits of anxiousness. When the blood pumping at however many beats per minute forced her into the present. Amber turned red again. Maybe it was the wine this time. Was she even allowed to exist as a person here? Take up space and live? She wasn't sure she'd feel comfortable doing that. What if they thought she was weird? A narc. God, how Amber hated making new friends. Would this proximity make it easier? Or just escalate the stakes? Amber wanted to drive a race ace car, or go for a run. Wow ow o, she was already not-tipsy, but not-not-tipsy from just the one glass of red.

Amber chewed slowly, the way you chew when you're trying to match the pace of the eaters around you, or when you want to chew soundlessly, but wind up heightening the mouth sounds of spit and food bits smushing and smacking into enamel, anyway. Her stomach was an animal. But for now, it felt like a tiger temporarily tamed.

She wasn't sure if she should say anything to break the silence. Or rather, the speechlessness. If she could be the easeful presence that charmed the room and changed the vibe for the better. Was it even her place to impose? Would they be grateful, or hate her? "Where are you from again?" She asked. "Natalia?"

"What'd you say?" Natalia said.

Why couldn't Amber enunciate and speak up? "Oh I know you're at Humboldt, but—?"

"She asked you where you are from, yes?" Alessandra translated.

"Oh, yeah. I was born in Italy, actually. But not really. My parents went to Lake Como for vacation before, and I was early. I came out—my mother gave birth to me three weeks early, so now I'm Italian. Kidding. Well, but we live in Berlin," Natalia said.

"Oh. That's cool? Where in Berlin?" Amber said.

"You've been?" Natalia said.

"No, I want to go, but—." Amber said.

"Oh, you must. It's— great. My family's in Mitte, which is boring and touristy, but it's only thirty minutes from Kreuzberg, which is where everyone at Uni lives. Not so bad," Natalia said.

"Do you, like, go to Berghain?" Amber had only said that because she wanted to prove that even though she'd never been to Berlin, herself, she was In The Know. That she knew about Cool, International things. But the second she finished voicing the question, her insides tightened, almost choking her stomach. She felt like swine, or regular, old butter: utterly uncultured.

Natalia said, "My favorite club was Chalet, but they closed, so now probably Salon Zur Wilden Renate, which is this—it's in a converted house, and now it's a circus—. You like to dance?"

Amber noticed that everyone else was finishing their food more quickly so she started to pick up the pace. She was used to being the fastest eater but here that didn't seem to be the case.

"I don't really go to—but I dance? Badly. I like to—. I clap on the offbeat. But I enjoy music," Amber said.

Natalia didn't smile; just pursed her lips and stared right into Amber's soul. It was the first time in a long while Amber hadn't felt anxious over space. Now she was anxious about how stupid she sounded, and how much she wanted to close the distance between herself and Natalia. How she wanted to just speak to her plainly plain lain, unthinkingly, truthfully. She hadn't wanted to confess her thoughts to anyone in a long time. She even found sharing her mental loops with her therapist to be draining and not exhilarating, but there was something about the curve of Natalia's eyebrows—no, the depth of her eyes—were they green? Blue? Brown? Grey? Amber suspected they were all of the colors; that's what they seemed to be from across the table—there was something about Natalia that made her crave.

"Alessandra, parla loro del festival," Marco interrupted.

Amber wanted to bite Natalia's lip. Her stomach was shaking, holding itself in. And that feeling wasn't Amber's way of waxing poetic or explaining "stomach butterflies" in a way her middle school self couldn't have dreamt up. That's just how it felt. It wasn't a pretty feeling.

"Ah yes, there will be a music festival in the woods near here soon. Electronic music at night, lots of people come in. It will be great. How long are you here for again? I forget these things. You may still be here," Alessandra said.

Amber looked like the dogs in Alessandra's car's headlights, barking mad and overwhelmed. Her stomach felt full, but in that way that carbs were overwhelmingly filling until they burned off in a flash. She was always stuffed by them, and then starving for more.

There was no healthy medium.

"We should go. If you're still around." Natalia said.

"Yeah, that'd be—that's so—that there's a festival here. Does it happen every year?" Amber said.

"For a few years now, in the summer. Lots of people, they come from all over," Alessandra said.

Natalia stood and fluttered over to the kitchen counter, bowl-in-hand. She asked Amber, "Have you finished?"

"Oh no, I—yeah." Natalia picked up Amber's plate. Amber stood to help but Natalia placed her arm on Amber's shoulder, instructing her to stay seated. Natalia tore one paper towel from the roll and gently scraped off Amber's leftover food from the bowl. Once their dishes were emptied and placed in the sink, Natalia sat back down on her stool and refilled her glass of water.

Alessandra said, "Tomorrow. We will have coffee and toast with jams at seven, and at seven-thirty Marco can show you the work. If you get hungry, please do help us finish the apricots. They just rot, so please, eat, eat, eat."

Marco downed the remaining half-sip of his glass of wine and closed his eyes.

He cleared the table while Alessandra washed the dishes. Lemon-scented dish soap ate away at the food remnants, feasting and making those untouched calories indigestible. Pots and pans clanking, scalding water cleansing—an artificial waterfall. The dishwasher beeped alive, began to run.

Alessandra explained where the DVDs were, should Amber want to watch a movie, since they really couldn't have her streaming content. "Remember, we pay for how much internet we use, so streaming and pictures, we have to pay for all this,"

They had films mostly from Italy, France, Germany, and America.

Natalia said, "Room in Rome was good. Luca and I watched it yesterday."

Alessandra said, yes, they had many good Italian films, but it was tricky for them, as they very much enjoyed foreign films, but it was difficult buying films in other languages, even English, as they hated dubbing, and would only buy foreign films which they could view with Italian subtitles, not a dubbed translation.

"It's harder to find the captioning in Italian. Everyone likes dubbing more, which is—. It makes it more tricky for us, you know?"

"Lei sa di doppiaggio?" Marco asked Alessandra.

Alessandra said, "Marco, sì, è americana, ma hanno il doppiaggio lì."

Marco responded, "No, lei sa perché non ci piace il doppiaggio qui in Italia? Anche se l'Italia sembra amare il doppiaggio?"

"Ah si, si," Alessandra translated, "Amber, do you know about dubbing?"

"I mean, I know what dubbing is?"

"It's fascist," Natalia said.

"Wait, really??" Amber wanted to count Natalia's freckles, but she had already been staring at her ever-transforming canvas of a face for far too long. The way that Natalia tensed her chin, or twitched her eyebrows, or nose, or mouth and her whole face was new again, like an Etch-A-Sketch. Amber remembered playing with one when she was little. How she could only manipulate two lines to make the picture, so whatever she created was always made up of the same stuff, but the images molded felt so drastically transformed. It's like saying two plus two is four. It's true, but two and two is completely different from four. Having two pairs of two—shoes, for example—is still the same as having four, but sometimes you need two as a unit, together. Two becoming one.

"Si, si. Mussolini was big with dubbing, so they could censor what we saw, you see? What we heard. This is why my parents didn't trust dubbing, and me, also," Alessandra said.

Amber recalled the episode of SpongeBob where worms have inhabited SpongeBob's sponge holes and he had to pretend he was normal, even though his body had quite literally become home to the animals. She imagined SpongeBob spewing pro-Italian government propaganda in his SpongeBob voice while little children watched, wide-eyed. Would he say "I'm READY—per facismo!" Would the children repeat his words, laughing?

"Anyway," Alessandra continued, "the WiFi is condito and the password is harrypotter, no caps or spaces. Luca wanted to be him when he was younger, so—it's fine for you to use, the WiFi, for emails, texts, Google, whatever. Just please, if you can, do not stream so much. Videos or pictures, they take up a lot of—we pay for what we use, and they use a lot, so if you cannot over—you know? This would be great."

Amber said she understood, and looked over at Natalia who seemed to have heard the spiel before. It's like she already knew the rhythms of the house. At this point, Amber presumed Natalia could function as the Podere's shadow government, quietly ruling the way it runs. The audacity of her clavicle. Amber realized she was thinking about Natalia's neck, which made her think of her own neck. She felt lightheaded and queasy and felt for her pulse. Did she have a fever? She felt flush. No one seemed to notice.

"We have *What We Do in the Shadows* and every film by Tarantino," Alessandra said.

"All the essentials," Natalia said.

Amber smiled politely, "Of course."

"Have you seen *Toni Erdmann*?" Natalia asked.

"I don't think so?" Amber said. Should she have seen *Toni Erdmann*?

Natalia plucked the film from the stack and handed it to Amber.

Alessandra said, "Remember, it's organized in alphabetical order."

Amber nodded, "Of course, I'll put it back where it came from."

And Alessandra and Marco said goodnight and headed off upstairs somewhere. To their room, presumably, perhaps to watch a movie with subtitles.

Amber had been so overwhelmed by the politics of the room; she didn't realize how much she had felt like an alien in a foreign landscape, trying to piece together their dynamics from their smallest actions. How quickly they sipped their wine or chugged their water. The way they moved and sat, sprawled out or confined on their stool seat. Who cleaned and cleared, the opportunism for leaving the table.

And now that everyone else had left the room, only these two relative strangers were left, biding time. Amber and Natalia, alone, surrounded by the relics of the family to which neither of them belonged.

Natalia reached over to the bowl in the center of the table and grabbed three apricots. She placed one between her lips, bit in to separate its flesh from the pit. "Why are you here?"

"Huh?"

"Why are you working on a vineyard?" Natalia asked.

"Why are you doing it?" Amber said.

"I'm only doing it because of my dad. He's friends with Marco back from when they were at Uni. And Marco was like, we need people to work, and my dad went to ask my brother, and I was like, uh, okay? What about me? Yeah, my ego is why I'm here, I guess," Natalia said.

"Oh, yeah. Do you like it here, though? Like, actually?" Amber didn't want their conversation to end, but she had to get to a bathroom really fucking fast.

Natalia shrugged her perfect shoulders. "I guess. It'd be nice to be paid, and not just work for room and board. I get room and board for no labor at home. Well, emotional labor, I guess. But you didn't answer."

"I wanted to travel, but that's expensive." Amber's stomach gurgled.

"They have pasta for dinner a lot. I think I miss vegetables more than I miss home," Natalia clearly heard her stomach's frustration. Fuck. Natalia continued, "So. Why did you want to travel?"

"Who doesn't want to travel?" Amber said.

"Yes, but why did you want to travel?" Natalia said.

Amber grabbed an apricot, and took a bite. This was not helping settle her stomach as she hoped it might. Natalia grabbed a few more from the endless stash which served as the boundary line separating the two girls. "I had a really, just like shitty year? And needed to escape."

Natalia nodded, and tore into the next bit of orangey fuzz.

"Are they always this quiet at dinner?" Amber asked.

"You thought it was quiet?" Natalia said.

Amber reddened, "Oh, I—"

"Marco doesn't trust his English," Natalia said.

"I can sort of speak Italian," Amber said.

"Can you?" Natalia asked.

"Not really," Amber said.

"That's all right," Natalia said.

"Are you —?" Amber said.

Natalia stared into Amber's heart. "Am I what?" A few heartbeats of voicelessness until Natalia said, "I'm gonna go watch a movie, I think."

Of course. "Of course." Of course she was going to watch a movie. "Night."

Natalia chucked her pits in the compost and left without a glance back.

Amber looked down dow do at the cloth clot lot placemat in front of her, marked by dried up crumbs crumb and crusty rusty rust eggplant sauce, crystallized. She counted to twenty-five, then got up and made her way to her room upstairs. The carbohydrates congealed in her stomach, making her queasy. She craved raved rave more ore or bread, or less fullness. Anything other than this empty togetherness, overstuffed loneliness.

She locked her door and went straight to her bathroom; she shut that door, as well. Hoping no one would hear her noise. She unzipped her jeans and pulled down her underwear. She sat down on the toilet seat. Her stomach was angry, but the food was not processed. It was still early on in the digestion process. And her stomach had been empty prior to dinner. She had nothing in her to shit out. But she needed to escape the stuff inside her. It contaminated her. She felt her body sweat and writhe. An alien particle had taken over control of her body. She pulled up her underwear, and got on her knees. She raised the toilet seat and let her body empty itself through her mouthhole, not her asshole.

Chunks of half-chewed penne and slimy hunks of eggplant snaked their way into the toilet water. She heaved until there was nothing but her own body inside her. She was shaking; her stomach ached. Her throat was too weak to scream—though it wanted to scream in pain. She looked herself in the mirror and wiped the vomit from her lips. She washed her hands and felt like a slut post-oral. She wondered where Charlie was right now. She closed her eyes and imagined his skinny dick. If she'd had any more substance inside her, it would've come up. But she was empty. And sore. Her eyes were bloodshot and tearing. She didn't want this? She was hungry. She was in Italy. There was so much she wanted to eat. To do. Consume. She didn't want everyone at the Podere to think she was bulimic. Or ruining their pipes. She hoped they hadn't heard her vomiting up their dinner. Would Alessandra be offended?

Amber brushed her teeth and her tongue. She used a fingernail to scrape the back of her tongue, near the bigger clumps of taste buds, not the smaller, bright red ones that seemed to elevate on occasion, trying to jump off, detaching itself from her muscle-fleshballofatongue. Near the part of her mouth she would press if she wanted to make herself gag, though she could never successfully make herself throw up. She could come close, gag and gag, but would never quite upchuck digested foodbits unless she was sick—and not just in the head. She hadn't made herself throw up, she assured herself of that. But had she? Did she want to be sick?

She gagged twice while she tried to get the gunky-yellow grime off her tongue. She only picked at the back bits of her tongue a few times a year. It always made her mouth taste rancid. She liked that taste, of feeling spoiled. Rotten. She brushed her teeth again to wipe her mouth fresh and clean. Washed over with a fresh breath of mint. Only a whiff of bile and spit. She preferred the soured breath. It made her feel more real and alive, that reminder of death.

Amber grabbed her phone. The connection wasn't ideal: two bars, but barely. She checked her emails, deleting all the welcomed spam: the Google alerts, the recipes, the capitalistic encouragements, this time from Ritual and The Reformation, John and Hank Green's newsletter.

She could hear some action film playing in the next room. If she could hear them, they could likely hear her. She hoped they were somehow too enthralled with the film to notice.

Amber was too wiped to watch *Toni Erdmann.* Instead, she loaded Instagram despite Alessandra's request. But instead of loading her newsfeed, she clicked the search page and looked up "Luca Rizzo," and just like that, up popped Luca's account. It was private so Amber could only see his tiny, wannabe-artsy profile picture alongside his follower count: 263 followers; 113 followed; 72 posts. She wondered if there were any pictures of the vines or of the jam. Probably not. Probably just photos of him and his friends. This didn't even seem to be a finsta, just a private insta. Amber understood the politics of the finsta, she had one of her own. Though the finsta isn't even really private. It's as personal as the insta, just a different fraction of personality performed in a more private realm. Instead of posting the best of life, there she posted the funniest bits, self-deprecating anecdotes. It was there she pretended to be funny, to have a sense of humor. Something she knew she lacked. Her "humor" came from verbalizing her greatest insecurities. She typed in "Natalia," hoping to find something, but with no surname, it seemed a lost cause. Natalia Maloof and Natalia Houghton were the verified people. Natalia Meloni had blonde hair. There were two Natalia S's, who did not seem like the Natalia for whom she was searching. There was a Natalia's Pizzabar in FIDi, back in New York. She clicked the location, and was impressed by the looks of their pizzas. Grandma-style with the tiny pepperoni circles. She clicked into her Notes App and wrote down "Natalia's Pizzabar" so she would remember to check it out. But no luck finding her Natalia.

Next door they were definitely in the middle of watching some chase scene. The music had gotten very loud. She hadn't been invited to their movie moment, just assigned viewing homework. She didn't need Natalia to think she could just drop all plans of her own to watch whatever weird movie she recommended. She had better, more pressing things to do.

Amber clicked open Safari and typed in "origin of penne." She felt smart upon reading that its name originated from the Italian word for pen, "penna," which is what she had accidentally sleuthed anyway. The first search result also explained that the pasta was universally loved, and perfect for chunky sauces. From her first-hand, field experience, Amber could not disagree.

Oh, the music had gotten loud because—well, now Amber could hear wet sounds of sloppy kisses, licks. Not from the movie. They didn't have the tinny quality of non-corporeality.

Luca coming. Natalia laughing. She imagined Natalia smiling, mouth wide, cum on her face, like she'd just eaten one of those cream puffs from Beard Papa's on Broadway and 77th. Amber's 8th grade after-school snack. A shell of soft pastry whose hole was stuffed, broken open with plush lightness. Whipped sugar and cream, vanilla extract.

White cream smeared all over, Natalia using her hands to wipe its excess into her mouth, filling her body with superfluous, caloric nothingness—the sweet, almost expired taste of salt. That's how Amber fell asleep, imagining. She was there with them, too.

Amber's alarm sounded, and she pushed herself up, out of the canopy of the covers. She did a full body scan, processing what had to be done before she was in working order, an automaton awakened. She kept on her shirt and threw on her overalls.

Alessandra hadn't said anything about laundry. She wondered if they'd let her use their machine when she needed it or if she'd be forced to utilize the sink as cleaning device.

She mechanically slipped into her boring, black Nike running sneakers. Her socks were already on her feet. Would they be enough to withstand the fields? Probably. And besides, what other option was there at this point? There was no Lady Foot Locker in Trevinano. Who felt that Foot Locker needed a Lady's edition? And who named it Lady and not Woman? Or Female? Or Feminine Foot Locker? Her foot wasn't a Lady. She was barely a Lady. Foot Locker for Ladies would be a more apt title for the place, though she'd probably not frequent the joint herself. Her feet were not feminine; they were grotesque. She liked them that way. Why couldn't women just use the Foot Locker? Who names a place Foot Locker anyway? Shouldn't it be Shoe Locker? Did they just mean for it to reference a gym locker, but specifically for feet? A safe space for Quentin Tarantino's sort of locker-room talk. Feet detached from their humans. Kept, and maybe frozen, or preserved with formaldehyde. Amputated feet. Some spares—rights or lefts, abandoned by their still-in-use other half—the other whole foot.

Amber supposed feet were the perfect example of a two plus two scenario, where the pair feels decidedly different than any mismatched two. Two of the abandoned locker-room feet could be mismatched. Two lefts don't make anything right, just as two rights don't leave one with any lefts.

Would the feet be naked? Socked or shoed? Would there be corns or blisters? Would they be untouched or even bound?

Shoe stores probably display, what, fifty to one hundred shoes? And they had to have more stock than that in back. Imagine. 500 feet, waiting for viewing. A foot fetishist's or necrophiliac's candy shop. Hairy, wrinkly, walked-on feet with high or flat arches. Insoles and pointe scars. Curled toes, painted nails, toe jam galore.

Amber never understood the allure of feet, but her high school boyfriend had passively mentioned that he didn't not find them hot, which is the only way to admit you have a foot fetish without admitting you have a foot fetish. So, she jacked him off one time with her two bare feet, using them like hands. She couldn't finish him off that way though; they were flexible and fast, but not so effective. She wound up sucking him off, but while she was doing so all she kept thinking of was how she wasn't just sucking his dick, but was also sucking the dirt from the bottom of her feet off his dick. The next time she took a bath after that, she tried sucking her big toe. It was boney and tasted kind of like her underpants smelled. Sweet and moldy, like the lotion she used to like.

She flung out a wad of spearmint toothpaste and spit in the sink, then ran the water to clean off the brush's germy bristles.

Natalia was downstairs already. She nursed a mug of espresso and nibbled at a thick slice of last night's bread, coated in a golden, coagulated jam.

"Morning! Coffee?" Natalia said.

Amber nodded. "Do you know where the mugs are?"

"Over there," Natalia swerved her neck, showing Amber the way.

Amber grabbed a mug, only to discover a chip on its rim. She was sticking with it—didn't want to look ridiculous and crazy, like she was the type of person who would be concerned about clay getting into her coffee, and being slowly poisoned by lead.

Natalia poured her two espresso shots worth of fluid from the Moka pot.

"Marco made the coffee earlier," Natalia said.

"Is that a warning?" Amber asked.

"No, it's just espresso," Natalia said.

"Ah."

"Do you prefer espresso or American coffee?" Natalia said.

"Both are fine, I guess," Amber said.

"You don't have a preference?" Natalia said.

"I mean, I love cappuccinos. But, when drinking just, like, plain espresso—I don't know, I like drinking coffee? I never want to finish drinking coffee? So, I guess it's nice when there's more of it? So, it takes longer?" Amber hated that she said all that.

Natalia's eyes blazed, all fired up, "Yes. This is—they think I'm crazy. What I've been doing in the mornings when I get up first, I use one of their larger kettles, which is really for twelve people, but I don't fill up the grounds. I put in less coffee but all the water, you know? And then it's practically like an Americano. But they don't understand. They think I'm just out here drinking twelve shots of—they don't get the appeal. Do you only drink in the morning? Coffee?"

"I usually drink like a cup or two in the morning, then another in the afternoon," Amber said.

"That's great news! At lunch we'll make Americano coffee," Natalia said.

Wow, honestly, Amber was impressed with herself. She was conversing like a normal, human person. From the outside she seemed chill and cool? "Cool! Sounds good." Don't blow this, Amber, she kept repeating to herself.

Natalia grabbed a couple apricots, "You should eat something."

Fuck. She heard. "Yeah, I'm starving."

"Are you feeling all right? I don't mean to pry," Natalia said.

"Oh. Yeah. I've just—if you—I'm sorry if—." Amber said.

"I used to be anorexic," Natalia said.

"Oh no, I'm not," Amber said.

"We don't have to talk about it, if you don't want to," Natalia said.

Amber nodded, "Is that the apricot jam?" Amber stared at Natalia's toast.

"No, Marco brought out the fig jam earlier," Natalia said.

"I don't think I've ever had fig jam before," Amber said.

Amber grabbed a couple of apricots for herself, and ate them in quiet. She had always been too much of a hypochondriac to ever be suicidal—she felt she couldn't worry so much about dying if she wanted to die—but in that moment, she didn't really care why she couldn't seem to retain food in her body, and all she wanted was for her existence to end, and for no one to notice.

Moments passed. The girls dumped their food waste into the compost and met Marco outside. They walked to the older vineyard, the one attached to the property. Marco explained how they had the old vineyard, the baby vineyard, and then the other one, which was small and didn't matter much, but they had it and the girls would probably have to comb those vines once they finished combing the vines in the old vineyard.

Natalia showed Amber how to comb the vines, which basically involved taking each individual vine—which grew from the ground and was supported upright by wirelines, which were, in turn, supported by small wooden bannisters, stuck into the ground—and gently wrapping it horizontally around the tallest wire it could reach, twirling it gently, but as many times as possible, so as not to rip or harm the plant, but to encourage it to latch on and continue its growth and attachment. Amber understood why this work was called combing. A sort of detangling and reorganizing. Except her hands were the comb; her fingers, its teeth.

Natalia twirled a few and Amber tried her hand at one. Marco corrected her, instructing her to wrap it around even more than she already had been doing. Once satisfied with her work, Marco headed for the baby vineyard where he and some boys from town would irrigate the land so the new vines would not die during this dry period. It was only then that Amber realized the air wasn't trying to suffocate her here. It wasn't stiflingly sweaty. Perhaps that would change come the afternoon.

She liked waking up early and getting a head start. The sooner she accomplished her daily tasks, the sooner her mind would stop yelling at her, reminding her of her human insufficiencies. It'd be so much easier if she were a robot and could just complete what was required without the insufferable anxiousness that came with modern existence.

Amber didn't believe neurotypical people existed anymore. They were the modern-day unicorns, a mere myth. That's why when that guy asked her what it was like, being anxious, Amber simply couldn't imagine planet earth without worry. Isn't life necessitated by fear of death? Amber's glorification of death only served to challenge the immense pressure she had placed on her own life. She had disavowed the unifying fear so as to allow herself reprieve from constant frenzy. How she hated that word: frenzy. It boiled her blood, made her feel like a witch. Made her feel like a female, a woman, a lady, a foot—her two feet snug inside her white and grey ankle socks, inside of Nike sneakers her podiatrist had prescribed to her after calling her Stan Smiths "utterly unsupportive," like they were a bad boyfriend, and not simply spineless foot-coverings.

It's funny: the night prior, when Alessandra rationed dinner and said Natalia and Amber needed less food for life—because of their gender—it would have thrown her on a bender, had she been home.

She hated—she liked to think of the end. After she used up all her spare time, she would be a body, a carcass. Remains divorced from sexual objectification. That was why she hated to be perceived. She didn't want. If no one could see her—.

Amber noticed Natalia put on her headphones. She wanted to talk to her once more before she wouldn't hear her. "We work till noon, right?"

"Yeah, then again at like five till six or seven-ish," Natalia said.

"Cool, cool."

Amber put on her headphones, as well. And then her stomach turned, and she rushed for the non-vine bushes lining the vineyard, retching, bent over, trying not to stain her sneakers, or hit her body with her own regurgitate. Her back arched, a black cat ready to scare, ridding her body of anything nutritious, staining her flesh with acidic resistance to her own existence. Her teeth felt filmy, her throat burned, her eyes. Why was she crying?

Amber slid the back of her wrist against her mouth, a surrogate napkin. She turned around, back toward the vines, and there was Natalia. Standing there watching.

"Can we talk about this?" Natalia said.

Amber's face became all twisted, and Etch-A-Sketched over. Why the fuck was she crying, this was—there was nothing to cry about. Deep breaths.

"I'm not—I swear, I'm not trying to do this," Amber said.

"Amber, it's okay. I'm not—I'm not, like, judging you," Natalia said.

"I'm not bulimic. If I was bulimic, I would at least be able to convince my mind to eat something. I haven't been able to keep anything down since I left the states. I am starving. I just—I don't know. My stomach is rejecting—I don't know," Amber said.

"Okay, okay, don't worry. I believe you," Natalia edged closer to Amber. "You're shaking."

"Yeah."

"Do you want to try and eat something?" Natalia said.

"My throat hurts so much. If I throw up again—." Amber said.

Natalia nodded, and asked if Amber wanted water or tea, something to soothe her throat. Amber assured her she was fine, and that she just wanted to be outside and do work for a bit.

Soundlessly, they combed. Amber's hands worked stems around coarse wires. Most of the stems were supple still, but some had already hardened and become wood-like. The leaves added weight to the movements. Dark, veiny surfaces shaded the stems from the sun, this is what Amber had to correct. She needed to expose their fleshy bodies to the light so they could grow.

She jumped back the first time she almost walked straight into a giant spider. Furry and brown, spotted, and smack in the center of two rows of vines. It would have landed right on the center of her face. She had to laugh. She was fine.

She carefully placed each of the stems and manipulated the leaves so they would not tear.

She couldn't imagine eating them. They seemed so—leafy. She wondered at what stage of growth they were harvested for stuffing. Could you consume any grape leaf? Or was there a particular Mediterranean grape that was most ripe for filling with rice, meat, spice, and heat. She imagined steaming the vines in their entirety. Make some great grape soup.

She wished the grapes had grown already, so they could harvest them. And she could swallow them. Eat something, and keep it down. Trap it in her body, and make it one with her. Make it part of her. Use its existence to aid her own.

When she was younger, she wanted to be Lucille Ball. She did a presentation on her in fourth grade, where she dressed up as Lucy and reenacted the chocolates scene. Where Lucy and Ethel work at the factory and can't keep pace, so they stuff their faces, and eat all of the chocolates.

Amber brought a box of assorted chocolates into class and ate them all while wearing a chef's hat. That was her presentation. Her homework. But that was playtime.

Now she imagined herself as Lucy in the grape-stomping episode. She wanted to feel the grape bodies squish and mush under the pressure of her feet. To dance on them and feel their guts burst and separate from their skins. To be made uncomfortable, to never be able to drink wine again. She wanted her body to pressure the grapes, to make them move and meld in ways they didn't want to. Force them to spill out liquids, liquids that would ferment. Fermented grape guts. She could picture Charlie guzzling wine. She wanted to make the wine that he would guzzle. To make him black out. To make the wine that would fuck him up. To naturally drug him, without his knowledge of her involvement. Was that illegal? Working on a vineyard. Making wine. Selling wine. Hoping he bought and consumed the wine. Blacked out on the wine. Got fucked up on the wine. Was it illegal? Her wanting power?

Her hands became filmy from dirt. Occasionally she'd spot a miniature bunch of unripe grapes, hidden beneath layers of leaves. Some of the vines were tall and thriving, others were young and supple, craving nutrients and water, sunlight. She tried to aid them on their journey, but broke a few, while turning them around and around the wire. There were some big spiders, too. Waiting for her on leaves, or even dangling between the rows of vines. Daring her not to watch her step, to walk right into their net, and break their home, become their prey. She prayed she would not fall into this trap. She ran out of podcasts almost immediately. She hadn't yet downloaded any audiobooks, so she played Sufjan Stevens and bopped to his tunes, fully living out her *Call Me by Your Name* fantasy. She still found it so unfair that the sequel, *Find Me,* was so straight, and not as good. But how do you follow up that epic romance?

The minutes felt like hours, but the work was steadying and pleasant. The sun rose and beat into her skin, but not in a way that irritated her paleness. The sun nourished her in a way soothed her vitamin D deficiency. She felt like a person who could help the world prosper. Even if that meant making wine, or helping someone else do so.

A tap on her back. She looked back and found Natalia.

"Hey?"

Natalia extended her hand, and offered Amber a few apricots. "I always bring a stash."

"Oh. Thanks," Amber said.

"You don't have to eat them. I just thought—. How are you doing?" Natalia said.

"Pretty okay. I like the combing." Amber felt a fool.

"Yeah, it's nice," Natalia said.

"Have you just been doing this for three weeks?" Amber said.

"No, different things. We just started combing this week. First, he had me remove the lateral shoots," Natalia said.

"The what?"

"Basically, all the parts of the vine that were growing, but like just wasting space and resources, not actually contributing anything. If anything, just blocking light and preventing the, you know, the rest of the vine to—."

"Stealing the spotlight?" Amber asked.

"Exactly," Natalia said.

"Interesting," Amber said.

"Yes, so Marco said it was very important for me to do that before we got to the combing, since it makes it easier. Some of the vines were very knotty? Knotted together? I felt bad, cutting life from the stalk. But I guess that life was so alive it was suffocating?" Natalia said.

Neither of them knew how to go on from here.

"That's kind of bleak?" Amber said finally.

"Yeah, when I said it—it felt bleak? But it wasn't at the time. They were just, the little, you know the little mini legs of the vine, the ones that grow and twirl specifically onto the wire? Like this?" Natalia directed Amber's line of sight to a perfectly, tightly wound spiral, which was, indeed clinging around the wire, contorting its body to wrap itself around the wire.

"Talk about attachment issues," Amber said, joking.

"But imagine—this small, little vine hugging so closely, reconfiguring its own self so it could hug more deeply this other vine? So close that it's suffocating, and debilitating. Like neither vine can grow straight up now, they're attached? They're conjoined. They're wrecking each other," Natalia said.

"It's like in an airplane," Amber said.

"Huh?"

"With the oxygen masks," Amber couldn't believe this was her analogy. "You know how you're supposed to put your oxygen mask on before you put your kid's mask on. Not that you—or I?— have a kid, but, like, hypothetically. You're supposed to save yourself, then help whoever else."

"Mhm—no, yes, exactly. That's exactly what—because, I felt bad? You know, breaking these vines apart, having to even kill— chop off some of their branches? To prepare the vines for *the combing*," Natalia said "the combing" in a way that made Amber feel like less of an idiot for using the official term. They were in on the same joke.

"I like it. The combing, I mean," Amber said.

"Yeah, this feels methodical. Next won't be as fun. Once we finish this," Natalia said.

"What're we doing when we finish this?" Amber asked, as she squatted down and pushed her back into a curve, stretching it out. She cleared the hair from her face with the back of her hand.

"Oh, just weeding, I think. It's so funny doing this. When I was little, I couldn't have conversations when I ate because, I don't know what it was, my imagination? But if I ate any produce I would be out of my body, kind of? I would be transported to the fields," Natalia said.

"Like dissociated?" Amber said.

Natalia said, "Yes, but not really. It happened with animals, too. I was vegan for the longest time because I'd have these terrible nightmares at the dinner table while awake. I'd eat a chicken and be trapped in a tiny cage, covered in my own shit. Because that happens. They have to live in their shit, their whole— they have to live through such—"

"I knew it was bad, but—"

"Yes, but then I realized if I ate cruelty-free animal products I would visit the nice farms and not the cruel ones in my sleep. It's the same as eating plants in that way. This must sound insane. I was a child," Natalia said.

"When did it stop?" Amber said.

"It's not that it stopped ever, I just stopped noticing it. It's like how you stop hearing sounds when they've been playing for a while," Natalia said.

Amber nodded, unsure what to say. This girl was weird as hell, which only made her fall all the harder. Amber stood back up and grabbed her phone from her pocket: only two more hours till lunch. Vine after vine, around the wires in circles, and circles. Moving big masses of conjoined vines, together, trying not to break even their edges. Trying not to make them snap. It was so easy to snap. So easy to end the life of each vine. Or slowly kill them. To be careless in the work was to ceaselessly murder. Amber was no murderer; she took her time. She waited for the spiders to move from the grand greenery, jutting straight up above her head. Once they'd catapult themselves to some other part of their web, she'd try to move the vine without breaking anything.

Everything in her life was about reducing her impact. To take up just the 5 feet 5 inches with a 28-inch waist line, and exist only as her physical form. To use her body to move vines and make wine. Her veins were throbbing. It must be the sun which was rising higher in the sky. Maybe it was the altitude. Or the work. Her jeans felt filmy like her hands. Thickened and calloused, used by nature for work.

Alessandra silently circled the premises to get her steps in, Natalia repeated lines from her audiobook like a prayer for Amber and not for God, "Poor girls. The world fattens them on the promise of love. How badly they need it, and how little most of them will ever get."

"What's that from?" Amber chirped.

Natalia blushed as she said, "The Girls? It's about a cult. Like Charlie Manson."

"Oh, my mom got me that for Christmas," Amber said.

"I'm liking it a lot, what are you listening to?" Natalia said.

"Sufjan Stevens," Amber said.

Natalia cackled, and checked the time on her phone, "It's 11:52."

"Oh?" Amber said.

"Wanna head back in now and just walk slowly?" Natalia said.

Amber nodded, and together they walked slowly back to the house, savoring the feeling of workless motion.

"Are you hungry?" Natalia said.

"Starving," Amber said as her stomach sunk. She felt pressured to keep talking but she didn't know what to say, so wound up asking what'd she'd been wondering since the night prior.

"Are you and Luca—?"

"Are we—?"

"You know," Amber said.

"He's a sweet boy," Natalia said.

"If someone said that about me, I think I'd have to die," Amber said.

"No!! It's—he's sweet. You'll see. It gets dull being here with nothing to do but work and shower and sleep and eat," Natalia said.

"Yeah, sometimes you just need a hobby. Something to do. Someone to do," Amber said.

Back at the house, they politely parted ways, going to their rooms.

Amber shut her door behind her with such vigor and she apologized to no one.

She took off her shoes, whose color had faded from black to dusty more quickly than she had anticipated. Blades of grass and clumps of dirt and muck had invaded the insides, thankfully not reaching through to her socks, which had already grown unclean and crispy.

She plugged in her phone to charge before she forgot. She changed out of her clothing and stood in the nude. The window swung open, and she was surprised again gain by her he view of the grounds. She shut the shades and turned the fan on.

Amber was so sweaty and disgusting. Her clothes were muddied and work-worn and she couldn't imagine eating food like this— let alone working another few hours. She looked in the mirror which hung from fro the door, and felt her he stomach which was bloated past comfort, though completely unfilled. Her high-waisted underwear was clearly a size too small, or outgrown, and had left a line around the center enter of her stomach. She grasped her puffed-out flesh with her fingers and felt for fat, excited by excess energy she may have stored. She let go, allowing her collagen to do its work and bring ring everything back to normal again gain.

Amber was taking advantage of her youth.

She leaned close to the mirror and examined her face. She bit her lips and wrapped them around her teeth, biting down, hiding them from herself, stretching the rest of her facial skin. She examined the skin above her upper lip; admired her shadow mustache. She hadn't gotten her lips or brows threaded in over four months. She looked down at her chest to check and saw that, yes, her chest hair had grown back since its last pluck.

Amber had more than one chest hair air; she had loads of peach fuzz. But she had only this one so coarse and violently brown, equidistant from her nipples. She had spent pent pen en e hours ours our worrying whether or not no she'd forgotten to pluck luck it; worrying if her Charlie would make fun of her, even though he wasn't like that and wouldn't have. But even though he wasn't like that and wouldn't have, she recalled how she had agonized not only over her chest hair, her chain mail of higher testosterone, but also over her arm and leg hair, which grew so plentifully, and her armpit hair. When she shaved, they gave her ingrown hairs, which led her to her hyperventilating, panicking over maybe having cancer and her crying in the urgent care. She worried so much over her pubic hair. Her eyes fired up, mad at herself. Her hair was so nice to her, and yet made her so afraid of everyone who wasn't attached to it.

Her hair on her head, too. She kept pulling at it, pulling it out. Pulling out knots and knotting it up again. It was so much, her hair. It was so curly and drew so much attention, it made her exist in her space when she wanted to hide.

She wondered if she'd been acting suspicious. Shouldn't they question the story she was telling them? It was too easy. A nice, college student in want of work. And what was worse than their trust, was hers in them. Had she not learned?

She went to the shower, and played with dials, fiddling with the water temperature until it was hotter than comfortable, properly scalding, the ideal climate for brewing tea. The water cleansed the grime of work. Naturebits and pieces just fuzzy enough to cling on to her hair and stick to her sweat cascaded down and built up on the drain.

She dried herself off and collected the dirt from the shower, cleaning the shower of her filth. She changed into fresh clothes, and lay down on her bed. Her hair felt stringy. She wondered whether Italy had soft or hard water. She didn't remember the difference, but her hair would.

In their family's group chat, she texted her mother and father:

Morning luvs!
Just finished first bit of work for the day
All is well here they are nice and normal all is good xox

She then texted Emma:

Hey u!

DUDE

|—

just got to the city so much has happened

can I call???

Within seconds, they were on a FaceTime audio call, and Amber was asking, "oh my God, are you alright?" In response to Emma choked out, "Hey."

"Seriously, Emma, what's wrong? Are you okay? Why are you in the city?" Amber said.

"We broke up," Emma said.

"Shit," Amber said.

"She's been seeing this dyke who lives on the Upper East Side. So, I don't know? We were, like, dancing? And someone was like super cunty, and knew we were together and monogamous, and was like, oh, bitch, love to hear you're open now? Where's your bottom??? And I was like, uh? What? And then everything came out, and then I wound up on the train, and now I'm outside the Met like a fucking Blair Waldorf wannabe? And it's seven AM and I don't wanna go back to my apartment, 'cause she's there, and—." Emma had to pause for a slurry of hiccups, likely resulting from the combination of alcohol and crying. Once they passed, she continued, "it just really fucking hurts. And now I'm in fucking hell."

"Hun, it's—you're not in hell, everything's gonna be—"

"I meant the Upper East Side. My God?!" Emma said.

"Sorry, duh. Okay. Emma?"

"Yah?"

"This is—it sucks. But, it's better to know now."

"Honestly, is it? We have a lease."

"She cheated. I think it's on her to fill your room."

"My parents cosigned."

"Do you wanna stay roommates?"

"Fuck no."

"Can you find someone else?".

"Ugh I hate how you're so fucking practical."

"Sorry, I just—"

"No, it's—what I need to hear."

"You're on the Upper East Side right now?" Amber could tell that Emma was nodding from the sniffly-crying sounds she transmitted through the phone. "Okay. It's early there, no? I was gonna say go to, like, Cafe Sabarsky or Russ & Daughters and eat a big, fat breakfast, and just Venmo request me however much it is, but I don't think they're even open yet."

"Yeah, it's so early. I think I need to just go home," Emma said.

"I'm so sorry, Emma."

"Life's so shit."

"I mean, she has 'polyamory' in her twitter bio. I know it sucks, but like, don't take this personally."

"Okay, so I'm at the train," Emma said just before the call cut out.

Amber placed her phone on her stomach and stared at the ceiling. The fan. The crack in the paint right above her head on the ceiling. The black speck that could be just that: a black speck. Or it could be a bug, dead or alive.

She had wanted to tell Emma about everything. That she was settled at the vineyard now, and that she had met someone cool and kind. That she couldn't swallow food and keep it down. That she kept imagining her body using up her fat reserves, and how she kept clinging to her own body, feeling for her fat, trying to hold on to it, protect it from herself, from eating itself. She didn't want to die. She was trying not to freak out, she was really trying. But the image of her own, personal stores of fat cells, globs of white guck, clotting up the edges of her body, being used as sustenance because she couldn't seem to stomach Italian pasta. What a sick joke.

She could never remind Emma of when she had to sit back and watch her slowly try to die by self-imposed starvation. When Emma would buy a salad just to play around with it, moving each lemon-and-oil drenched piece of Sweetgreen-massaged kale, occasionally stabbing a chickpea or two and never actually swallowing, or even chewing anything, hoping no one was watching. Had she been seeking some sort of invisibility?? Would they ever be able to really talk about it? She remembered the first time Emma got so dizzy she almost fainted. How they breathed slowly together in unison and Amber yelled for Laney to find some orange juice or anything with sugar.

But Emma wouldn't shut up about how snatched she looked with her 24-inch waist line.

How the first time she fucked Allie and came to Amber's room sobbing, saying she felt disgusting? How Amber had to force feed her for the next week, to make sure she'd eat. How she felt like Hugh Grant's secretary in *Love Actually* with the 'tree trunk' thighs. And Amber looked down at her thighs beside hers. How she didn't want her tree trunks anymore. Amber's thighs were bigger. And when they cuddled, Emma called Amber cozy and Amber said thank you. And they ate popcorn and Emma cried.

Amber's insides blistered. Her intestines tightened—. She didn't have an eating disorder. But she felt like an alcoholic at an AA meeting saying she wasn't not an alcoholic. She didn't have an eating disorder. She was just— eating disorderedly. But she wasn't doing it on purpose. Does anyone eat disorderedly on purpose? Or does the world just unwilling shovel doctrines and diets down everyone's throat?

When Amber was little and would wake up scared by her dreams. she couldn't move. She remembered her eyes racing around, trying to calm herself down, but feeling trapped in the prison of her own skin. Sometimes, when she'd try to scream or call for her parents, she'd feel her throat catch on nothing. She'd feel pressure, like the room was a person, closing in on her, choking her whole body, whatever parts of her tried to move. To use the room's space. She'd stare at her walls, and try her hardest to think of nothing but the walls. She would stare at the layer upon layer of Sherwin Williams' Lazy Grey SW 6254.

Amber was the last to join the table for lunch. She scooted into her spot as Alessandra handed over to her a plate filled with fish sticks and fries. Alessandra kept the fresh cod and bed of greens for herself, Marco, and Luca. Normally this would have offended Amber, but she'd never been so grateful for half-a-plate of fried potatoes. Luca stole a handful of fries from Natalia's plate while she was preoccupied with watching Amber cautiously select a fry, perfectly crisped, chew and swallow.

Alessandra initiated chatter by saying to Amber, "The work is nice, yes?"

"Oh, yeah. It's beautiful." Amber couldn't resist smiling. She wasn't sure exactly why but she wanted to laugh. She restrained herself and found Natalia's gaze.

"Bene, bene. Natalia showed you all the, the ways? The tricks?" Marco said.

Amber released some spare laughter, and smiled, "Of course, of course."

Alessandra's attention shifted from the girls, to her boys. "Marco, Stefano è venuto? Il suo piede è guarito? Dimmi!"

Amber watched Natalia's face, trying to deduce her thoughts as Natalia bit into a fish stick. Amber couldn't discern that Natalia was thinking of the dinosaur-shaped chicken nuggets from her childhood. Natalia's father couldn't cook, and her mother was always traveling for work, so she grew up on a diet of bratwurst, dumplings, pizza, spätzle, and, yes, fish sticks, too. She only got a taste for cooking when she followed her best friend, Elisabetta, and her family to their home in Füssen for the summertime. Elisabetta was often recruited for family outings and social gatherings, so Natalia spent her days roaming and reading Nabokov, brewing coffee just for the ritual of it, watching onions caramelize and blacken, making pies, perfecting crust, inventing new recipes, and combinations. Her Guinness-cream-cheese-apple-pie-with-pecans was sublime. And disappeared before Elisabetta and Co. got home. Along with the evidence.

Only when Natalia caught Amber staring, did Amber look away.

Marco nodded dismissively and sated his wife saying, "Si, si, è venuto e ci ha aiutato. Ne abbiamo irrigato circa un terzo delle viti, si, Luca?"

"Si, pappa," Luca said.

Alessandra said, "Le previsioni dicono che stasera pioverà," Marco huffed, but she continued, "Si, caro, si. Natalia, Amber. If it rains later, you don't go to work, yes?"

The girls nodded amenably. Natalia casually moved her hand off the table and placed it onto Luca's thigh. Amber looked down to her plate. The fish sticks would not do. She searched for her next fry, seeking one not-so oversaturated with oil and crispy from heat and fat. She wanted a fry limp and soft, that would melt into her mouth and soothe her stomach, not poke and pester.

Amber only managed to swallow another four or five French fries before she felt her stomach turn, her throat clench, her chest tighten. She feverishly looked at Natalia, who was too busy eating off Luca's plate to notice Amber's look of I'm-being-held-captive-by-my-stomach-or-my-brain-or-my-stomach's-brain.

Amber was going to throw up.

She shot up from her seat, and carried her plate to the compost, where she emptied it before taking it to the sink.

"Finished?" Marco asked.

Alessandra jumped in saying, "You boys, all you do is eat, eat, eat. I'm telling you, us girls, we don't need so much."

The water gushed and splashed Amber. She quickly washed off her dirtied dishes, and placed them away in the dishwasher. It was only when she was about to offer kindly excuses for her prompt exit that Natalia finally looked up from Luca's plate. Seemingly disappointed, she asked, "No coffee?"

"Later," Amber squeaked out, ashamed by her own curtness. She decided a white lie was better than anything else she'd sputter out, "sorry to be so hurried, I told my mother I would call her."

"Of course, of course," Alessandra waved Amber off, before she added, "You have a phone plan? For international—you're not using WiFi?"

"Alessandra!" Marco said, before smiling apologetically and asking Amber to "Please tell your mother hello from us."

"Yes, I have a—" Amber smiled, as she abandoned ship.

Alessandra moved onto her next target for interrogation.

In the bathroom, Amber gagged; a cat expelling a hairball. But the fries wouldn't come up. Her body felt sick, like it was dying. Her brain was trying to keep it down, but her body was insisting the food was contaminator. Was she doing this to herself? She didn't want to die. She coughed and coughed, and felt herself go lightheaded. Would she suffocate to death? Was there puke in her lungs? She wanted to scream and cry. Could they hear her downstairs? She coughed up spit and air. She needed to expel her body of—some soft, white goo amounting to no more than a handful—a few French fries worth of vomit came up, hued brownish from the coffee, she presumed. Her body fell down to the tile floor, she caved into herself, sinking her body as low as it would go. She started to cry, a dry but physical cry. A soundless whimper. Or perhaps she was just shaking, afraid. There was a knock on the door.

"Hello? Amber? It's me," Natalia said.

Amber said, "Come in."

And so, Natalia did. Slowly, cautiously. "You okay?" Natalia said as she peaked into the bathroom, "You might wanna flush that."

"I wasn't sure if there was more," Amber said.

"You ate, like, three fries."

"Hey. I think I swallowed four."

"Look—"

"What?"

Natalia sat down on the tile floor, right beside Amber. "I know we don't know each other well or anything," Amber blushed, so Natalia hesitated, then said, "What?"

"Nothing."

"I can leave."

"No, I just, like, yeah, I barely know you."

"I'm not gonna judge you if you're bulimic.".

"You don't believe me?"

"I just don't know what I'm supposed to be believing."

"I'm afraid I'm gonna die here."

"What?".

"I feel like my whole world is crumbling before my eyes."

Natalia just nodded and stayed put, until she could take it no longer and she pulled out her phone.

"What are you doing?".

"I'm Googling."

"What're you Googling?"

"We're gonna figure out what you have. You say you're not bulimic. I believe you."

Amber found Natalia's belief in her to be frightening. So, she ignored it, and said, "I try not to use WebMD, it only makes things worse."

"Well, what? Do you want Alessandra to drive you to the hospital?"

Natalia asked.

Amber said, "Fine. What are you Googling?"

"Things like bulimia that are not bulimia," Natalia said.

"It's not even like bulimia at this point, I can barely eat at all. Let alone binge," Amber said.

"I think bulimia can involve mostly purging," Natalia said.

"Why are you helping me?" Amber said.

"You think Luca was going to?" Natalia said.

"You don't have to help me," Amber said.

"Amber, you can tell me if you are doing this to yourself," Natalia said.

But then Amber started to shake again, and cry. Natalia just sat there beside her. "I didn't mean to upset you. I'm sorry." Natalia paused, "Can I hug you?"

"I smell like puke. I'm disgusting," Amber said.

Natalia scooted closer to Amber, and held her from behind, wrapping her arms around her body; she was a human weighted blanket.

"You're fucking Luca," Amber said.

Natalia asked, "Jealous?"

Amber just nodded.

Natalia leaned in and whispered into her ear, "I know," before she rose to her feet and said, "I'm gonna do some sleuthing. Figure out what's plaguing you."

That afternoon it rained. The fog was thick and heavy, and blinded everything outside from view. The sky and the land looked the same from Amber's room. It was all grey and cloudy. She actually found it comforting, staring out there into the nothingness. It reminded her of the walls at home, Rick Riordan's repeated descriptions of Athena's striking grey eyes in all the *Percy Jackson* books, of the Nowhere dimension in that episode of SpongeBob where Squidward gets transported to the plain of pure nothingness, with only random panels of colors for companion. Pink and yellow panels demarcated some otherwise unseen and unfelt ceiling, and auburn and turquoise rectangles lined the floor, showing space. The word "alone" echoed to ensure his devolvement into the depths of insanity—. Amber remembered him running, searching for escape. For an edge or a border, a way out. She presumed he did escape, and find his way back to Bikini Bottom, but she couldn't recall how. She felt her feet on the floor, and looked upwards at the ceiling, with its cracks and dead bug?? All alone. Could she escape this? Did she want to?

Amber texted Emma, telling her about her body. She wrote her a novel of a text, explaining how she was worried she was doing this to herself, even though she didn't mean to. How she wanted to disappear. She wanted to break herself as others had. But, also, how she didn't want that at all? How the ways in which she wanted to break herself weren't by killing herself? And making herself tear up and sweat, her throat throb, her stomach ache, her mind go numb and feel so dumb, her hands were shaking even then as she typed—she felt so faint, but perhaps that was the altitude or the weather. Her breath felt funny, irregular. Her head felt like it was going to explode. Like there was too much pressure inside her skull. Like a hole needed to be cut into it, just so some spare air could be released. So she could make some space, some room to think. Everyone needs some room in one's own skull.

Emma texted back immediately, very concerned. She reiterated the concrete symptoms, and asked follow-up questions. She told Amber to stay hydrated, and try—really try—to keep down some nutrients. Some something.

Amber said she didn't have a death wish. So yes, she would heed her advice.

Emma texted back, asking if she'd ever watched *Diagnosis* on Netflix.

>   u rly recommending me my next binge rn?

nono no I —
there's an episode you should watch.
I forget what season but Allie loved the show
so she made me watch

>   ???ok?

there's a girl w this thing
sounds like
idk
like just watch the show

>   im not allowed to stream content here

what?

>   too much wifi

they have to pay for all the wifi we use what does she have?

>   in the show I mean
>   like what's the disease

ok im out rn heading to lunch w my mom
when I'm home will try and find it and text u

>   thx doc

ik ur like kidding or whatever, but text me
if anything I dunno if anything happens
This is scary???

>   dw dw
>   I'm fine

do ur parents know?

>   what ? No all is good all is good
>   truly truly

                                                    Oh !
                                                    Also!
What is it?

                                    I think the girl is into me
Omg! What happened?

                                    She like whispered in my ear
What?
Weird
                                         Nono it was like hot
? Ok
?!?!?!?!
                                    Like when I asked if they were like
                                                    Ducking
                                                    Ducking
                                                    Ducking
                                                       FUCK
                                                 FUCKING******

HAHHAHA lol
                                                    I'm an idiot
I gtg but this is insane girl
                                              R u really ok Emma ??
                                                    Ik u loved her

Get that dick
That hussy
Yah I —
Imma be ok
Spiraling but normal spiraling

Breakup spiraling

> LOL ok
>
> This is what you think of me I see
>
> luv you

Amber found herself standing in front of Natalia's door, ready to knock. She hadn't remembered making the decision to walk there, she had just followed her body's movements and arrived. Her mind was spinning and hurting. She couldn't think, so she didn't; she just knocked on the door.

"One second," Natalia called out before opening it. Her hair was wet. Stuck to her skin. Water pooled into beads that ran down her neck like raindrops or sweat. She was still pulling down her shirt.

"Sorry. I didn't mean to barge," Amber said.

Natalia waved Amber off and said, "Come on in," as she retreated back into her room. Amber followed a few paces behind. Natalia continued, "I was just gonna watch a movie, but Luca also mentioned—"

"It's nice that we get the afternoon off—"

"His friends might wanna hang later. You should come."

"Oh, I don't want to intrude or anything," Amber said.

"It's fine. We can intrude together. What's up?" Natalia said.

"Oh, nothing really," Amber said, feigning casualness, before getting back on track, "Sorry about coffee, about bailing."

"Are you okay?" Natalia said.

"I don't know what to do," Amber said.

"Here, sit down," Natalia guided Amber to her bed. "Do you want to talk about it?"

"I mean, you know already. It's nothing—I don't know what to do, and my friend Emma told me to watch this Netflix show to help me self-diagnose? And I'm just tired," Amber said.

"I mean, yeah, you don't have any energy inside you," Natalia said.

"No, I mean, that too, but emotionally, I'm exhausted," Amber said.

"What can I do? What do you want to do?" Natalia said.

Amber didn't respond.

Natalia sat down on the bed beside Amber and pulled her closer, wrapping her left arm around her body. She began softly stroking Amber's scalp with her right hand. Amber felt so safe she could die. But the feeling of security suddenly terrified her. She rose to her feet and apologized for being an imposition. Perhaps she was a misogynist for coming to her so unthinkingly.

Natalia waited for Amber's ramblings to lose steam and leave her without words, mind blank, noiseless. Amber stared at Natalia and awaited judgment that never came.

Instead, Natalia reached her arms up high toward the ceiling and stretched them backwards. She exclaimed, "God, it's humid. I'm sweating," and just like that she was pulling off her shirt, and exposing her braless chest. She looked so dewy. Like a soda can perspiring in the heat. Amber swallowed her spit. "Aren't you warm?"

Amber nodded.

"What's the show you mentioned?" Natalia said.

Amber's voice cracked as she said, "*Diagnosis.* It's on Netflix."

Natalia nodded and reached for her laptop, and within minutes had found the episode, and they were watching it side-by-side, sprawled out on the bed. And while they watched the sick American girl consume dinner with her family at the dinner table, spit bucket in-hand, Natalia said, "You don't mind if I take off my jeans, do you?"

Amber shook her head, no. The girl on the computer screen was gagging and running to the bathroom now. Natalia looked at Amber who looked at the girl, so concerned. Feeling called out. Seen.

She was convulsing. Saying that it just "Turns my stomach in a way where I just can't handle it. I haven't kept fluids down."

Natalia asked Amber, "Have you been keeping fluids down?"

"Trying to," Amber said.

And the TV girl said, "Whenever I throw up, I keep on eating just so I can get some calories in my stomach," and both Amber and Natalia nodded. Amber had been doing that. And the girl said how it feels like her head is going to explode. Amber turned rouge.

Natalia's hands were on Amber's cheeks, feeling her temperature, "You're burning up. How can you stand it?"

Amber realized she could stand it no longer so she pulled off her shirt, and shimmied out of her jeans. She was wearing only a bra and underwear now. Her nipples puckered because of the temperature, and she realized she hadn't plucked her nipple hairs, or shaved or trimmed any of her hair in a long while.

The girl on the screen breathed heavily as she explained how her breathing patterns are strange and irregular. How it'd been two months since something she'd consumed had stayed down for more than a few minutes or hours. How she'd lost nearly ten pounds. Amber saw her body beside Natalia's, and compared the size of their biceps. Hers were weak, and Natalia's looked strong, juicy.

"You can use my arm as a pillow. If you want," Natalia said.

"What?" Amber said.

"It seemed like you were looking at my arm, so I thought—."

Amber wished Natalia would speak forever. Her voice felt like honey, deep and secure, like it always knew what it wanted to say and how to say it. She was so certain.

The computer's fan revved up, trying to cool off the battery, or whatever was working overtime, getting hot sitting on Natalia's bare legs. Her room was made of all the same parts as Amber's. The same bed, the same dresser, even the same fan, only arranged slightly differently. It was uncanny, the slight differences. How the dresser in this room was to the right of the door, not to the left.

The walls were white. Painted pure, touched to look untouched. False.

The girl on *Diagnosis* was originally diagnosed with Postural Orthostatic Tachycardia Syndrome (POTS). They thought it was such because of her dehydration. Symptoms include heart palpitations, dizziness or lightheadedness, fainting. The nerves that control the blood vessels don't work right. It's a disease of the nervous system.

"Oh, shoot!"

When she stood, her heart rate—

"What is it?" Natalia asked.

Changed really quickly. From zero to one hundred.

"We're not supposed to stream movies, right?" Amber said.

Inhale. Natalia moved her head into the nook of Amber's neck. Exhale. Could Amber have POTS? Was that all this was? All this was? How serious was POTS? Could she repair all her blood vessels? All of her blood vessels: damaged. More damage: acquired. How to repair? More baggage: gotten. How to give? How to leave? Goodwill? Wherever? Breaths. Deep, deep breaths.

Natalia said, "They'll survive."

The doctor clearly thought the girl featured on *Diagnosis* had Rumination Syndrome, a rare chronic functional disorder, which involved the automatic spitting out or regurgitating of food after eating. A non-deliberate form of bulimia. Often triggered by injury, illness, or distress, resulting in the backwards flow of food from the stomach to mouth. Amber wondered if she'd puke up her stomach itself, an appendix, or maybe even her heart.

Natalia hugged Amber with her whole body. Amber had gone flush, as if she'd seen her own fate written in the stars before her eyes. Netflix was her oracle.

The neural pathways go haywire and get rewired; ridding the self of filling agents such as food and drink becomes part of the natural order of consumption. The mother didn't buy this diagnosis. The girl seemed more willing, but still didn't want to seek behavioral therapy in Milwaukee, at the only medical center equipped to deal with the syndrome. The backwards flow of food and thought.

Amber finally said something, asking, "Can you believe her mom?"

"Ridiculous." Neither of them knew what to say, so Natalia continued filling the quiet with noise, "Crazy that your friend just knew about this. I've never even heard of this show."

"Yeah, Emma's—."

"She's what?" Natalia said.

"She loves the grotesque. And reality television. And this kind of is both," Amber said.

"How are you doing?" Natalia said.

"I'm okay. I don't know what to do. Like, do I need to go to Milwaukee? Am I being like that girl's mom, but to myself by not just going? And making them treat me?" Amber asked.

"We don't even know this is what you have. And it hasn't been two months yet, it's been a few days," Natalia said.

Amber's voice caught in her throat before she could say anything in response. She moved out of Natalia's grasp, and put back on her shirt, and then her pants. She croaked out, "Do you think Luca's friends will be okay if I tag along? If you all wind up hanging out?"

Natalia assured her she would be most welcome to join, and said she'd let Amber know the plan as soon as she knew. Amber walked back to her room, like a zombie walking to her grave, but only for a nap, as she was already undead, or would be if she were a zombie.

She opened Messages and tried to write something back to Emma. She felt obliged to say thank you, but for what? For helping name her ailment? What good did that do? She felt ager and hopeless and helpless. Like nothing could fix her body so vexed by the world. She wanted to disappear and die. She wanted to throw up all of her insides. She kind of liked this disease. She felt empty, because she was. She contained nothing, and so she was nothing. She texted Emma:

> Duck
>
> Duck
>
> Fuck*

It was so random. Everything. What happened. How she got here. That Emma liked that random Netflix show. This all felt ordained. She felt it in her gut: this inevitability. What did she feel in her gut?? It was nothing, of course.

Amber opened a new message, and typed "Charlie." She had deleted all of their message exchanges from before, keeping only a few screenshots as record. Her fingers lingered over the keyboard, flirting with the boundless options of what she could type to him.

She typed:

> I could tell the people at Fulbright what you did

But she didn't press send. She just closed out of messages and opened Facebook. Her mother had posted a selfie at Tavern on the Green with the caption, "Go green in style!" What did that even mean? That was supposed to be eco-friendly, she presumed, but wound up sounding more elitist and environmentally-unfriendly than not.

She scrolled through more of Facebook, Instagram, and Twitter. She watched some TikTok videos and many Instagram Stories, and listened to some delirious SoundCloud music which involved screaming cries of "MOMMY! FUCK ME!!" with whale mating sounds and classical music as its backdrop. She felt sick on dopamine, so many hits and she still wasn't sated by the fix. She craved more and more content, more photos of hot Florida girls she hated in tiny pink bikini thirst traps, and pictures of lavish meals, and happy families and couples, sloppy pictures from the club, and Tweets about all the dick, cunt, and butt the kids were riding, eating, beating, and fucking.

@**edithwhoreton:** I'm in an Uber pool with a Birkin bag

    @**lacroixifixion:** I —

        @**edithwhoreton:** she's red snakeskin

@**drappleistheog:** for all of high school I think I just had a crush on a haircut

    @**edithwhoreton:** I still have a crush on a haircut

    @**drappleistheog:** tea

@**lacroixifixion:** you either want to slap or be slapped

Amber closed her phone, and spacetime had changed. A content overdose.

Luca's friends were a bunch of uglyhot Italian bros who'd read Marx once and thought they were smarter than everyone else because of it. They were at his friend Antonio's house, which was this insanely large Podere with a breathtaking view of Umbria, Tuscany, and Lazio. A castle on the hill. Everyone was either in the pool or lounging around, cracking open beers and eating slowly rotting apricots and small, green pears freshly fallen from the tree. The air was made sweet and smokey by the alcohol and fruit, and cigarette smoke everywhere.

Some boy who neither Natalia nor Amber had met yet, joined the party bearing an unopened bottle of overpriced whiskey. Before they knew it, everyone was taking shots, chanting for everyone to drink more, more, more until it was all gone. Amber was drinking and felt so lightheaded and dizzy, like she could do anything. She was in the pool next to Natalia. With no food in her stomach to absorb the alcohol, she became very, very, veryvery intoxicated. Straight-up drunk. She excused herself and made her way to the bathroom where she threw up all she'd drunk, which somehow made her feel even drunker. She looked at herself in the mirror and didn't recognize her own image. She smiled at herself, and fixed her hair before swaying slowly back to the pool.

When she arrived, Luca and a couple of his friends were jumping in, butt-naked. Laughter and jeers. Natalia shrieked. The boys hung off of her. Amber sat criss-cross-applesauced on the ground beside the pool and watched the scene play out from a distance. She felt like she pressed play on a simulation and was now living in virtual reality.

She got distracted by the rush of the man-made waves and the sound of the cicadas. She put her feet in the water and moved them slowly, methodically, entranced by how they changed the way of the water. When she looked up, everyone seemed closer together—bodies on bodies, so close, connecting—becoming an orgy in the pool in the Italian countryside. Could she be dreaming this all up in her head? Her friends had gone to plenty of orgies, but they were always organized and kinky and gay. People made wristbands explaining to what they consented. She had friends who had been to the baths, and were fucked by hundreds of men, but that was a space designated for such. This was just—as if Natalia were the Earth's core, her gravity pulled Amber from the ness into the wet water—the throbbing center of the loch. Amber waded her way through, took off her swimsuit, getting completely nude.

She passed by all the boys, there had to be five or six, all trying to feel or kiss Natalia, to hold her. Amber walked straight up to her and they kissed. And, of course, the boys reacted; they loved it, but Amber and Natalia didn't even care; they just kissed for what felt like forever, if forever could be too-quick and an instant. And all of a sudden, they were inside—Amber was lightheaded. Time acted strangely. Natalia grabbed her hand, and the boys were fucking them both, as they lay beside each other on a large bed.

Amber moved someone's dick from her cunt to her ass, "I've always wanted to try." She felt like she was reverse-defecating, like she was eating through her butt. She wondered if dick-absorbing would make her throw up. "Slower," she instructed. It hurt, but it was kind of hot. She liked the idea that she was so kinky. She wondered what Natalia thought of her right then, so she looked, and saw that Natalia had been staring at her, perhaps for this whole time. She smiled, and wanted to cry.

Natalia mouthed to her, "Hey, you."

Amber blushed, and wanted to say everything, but had no words, and just then was flipped to her side, and someone came into her cunt. And she was filled: hole and hole. Vagina and anus. Her whole body was just holes: mouthhole, butthole, peehole, earholes, noseholes, holes between her fleshmolecules. Perhaps she wasn't a girl or a young woman after all. Perhaps she was like all people, just a hole, or a collection of holes, in need of filling and fulfillment. Or perhaps she was just another sponge, ready to absorb all the chaos life would offer her for the sake of easily repeatable, beloved stories. Perhaps she lived her life to produce good content for other people's consumption. Her life was narrative, or felt like that when she was dissociating. This was a good story. The spontaneous orgy in the Italian countryside. One of the boys was cumming inside her cunt. She didn't know how to say "pull out" in Italian. "C'est la vie," she thought. "Or è la vita? Italians probably said C'est la vie just like Americans did. Like the French do." Right? She wasn't making sense, even to herself.

She realized she was turned over on her side for ease of this sexual hole-filling, but she could no longer see Natalia, and their hands had separated.

If this were recorded, would it be listed as "gangbang" or "glory hole" on PornHub? She wanted to throw up but there was nothing left inside her. She had nothing to throw up. It would probably be listed as "two sisters get gang banged together." She wondered if she found sister porn hot because she didn't have a sister. If having a sister would make it weird. It was probably weird already, even though she didn't have a sister. At least siblings of the same sex couldn't procreate and fuck up a child. Aren't all children fucked up, though? The world fucks you, if your parents don't. Figuratively, though she supposed literally, as well. Imagining herself as the lead of a PornHub video made everything feel hotter. She imagined she would have a 63% approval rating; who knew what people would write in the comments.

> lol imagien if she marrys 1 day
>> she has a bf no?
>>> he's prob jacking off to this rn

> I think she's single
>
> fuuuuuuuuuck
>
> my god I think I've seen god, but also where is god?
>
> lol this comment has me lol-ing and also cummingggggg
>
> this is disgusting I am a xhristian
>
> wanna mingle?
>
> that guy came so quick whoa her pussy must b dank
>
> her butt at 4:37

It was kind of hot. She wanted to cum. She hadn't in a while.

 She tugged at the balls of the guy in her cunt, and she tried to get him off, and he came, and at some point, the guy up her butt had also left her alone with her body. Her holes ached as she watched the boys still suckling on Natalia's teats, and licking her cunt and eating her ass. In middle school, George M. would always read comments from PornHub aloud during lunchtime while Joe L. would ask girls if they watched porn. Amber remembers lying and saying she did. He may have asked what kind, but she doesn't remember for certain if he did, or what she replied if he had.

She was dying from being alive. Malnutrition, dehydration, panic, fear.

She didn't have to be born, or even survive. It was a miracle. She could have killed herself at any point in her lifetime. Perhaps she would have if she hadn't been so concerned with all the ways she may die.

The guy pulled out, and a new cock came for her empty mouth-hole.

She pushed it away, and felt her stomach contract. She curled into herself, and looked at her chest.

Some guy groaned. Must have felt good. She was so blotchy. Even her arm hairs were on edge. The beer and whiskey foamed in her mouth, she searched for somewhere to spit it out. No one noticed.

She wanted to hide, but was already hiding: in plain view. She was so embarrassed. The walls were wooden, and confining. Poplar wood, surely. She took a woodshop class in elementary school. She had made a twelve-inch model of a tugboat and painted it primary colors. Then she made a stool for herself and painted it grey.

The guy came for her mouth again. She let him, opening wide, letting her upward flowing fluids expel onto him. He backed off, saying something she didn't hear. Everything went fuzzy.

Grey, grey, grey. One day her hair will turn grey. Salt-and-pepper.

Natalia caught Amber's eye and said to the young men who still scavenged her young body for their pleasure, "Okay, okay, okay! Shoo, shoo! Go, go! Boys, out of the bed!!!" And they listened to her?? They got out of the bed. And Natalia continued saying, "Now Amber and I get to have a turn." The boys cheered and expressed their disappointment at not being able to watch. Natalia followed them out and locked the door in their wake.

The room became so quiet with just the two of them in it. Natalia got back on the bed where she and Amber laughed, or maybe cried.

"This is not what I expected," Amber said.

"Me either," Natalia held Amber's head between her hands and asked, "Can I kiss you?"

Amber's heart beat so quickly her vision was going purple. She nodded so quickly that they both did that breathy half-laugh that happens when two people in lust finally drop the bit and just make-the-fuck-out. Natalia bit Amber's tongue, and Amber bit Natalia's lip, and they were kissing each other's necks and ears and holding each other close.

"You're shivering," Natalia said, as she grabbed the covers and tried to warm Amber with the heat from her own body.

Amber's teeth chattered as she said, "Sorry." A knock on the door cut her off mid-word.

"Will you let me in?" Luca said from the other side of the door.

Natalia got up to let him in.

Luca came back inside the bedroom, though he didn't seem particularly interested in getting into bed with them. In fact, he seemed completely sobered up, like a parent picking up their kid from a playdate gone long. Amber wondered if Luca had just been fucking Natalia for most of the time, and if he felt jealous or uncomfortable being spit sisters now with all his friends. She didn't recall him ever coming close to her. Did he find her so unattractive? She didn't find him particularly attractive. He just happened to be there.

"Ready to head out?" Luca said.

"Already?" Natalia said.

"You two can do whatever back home," Luca said.

He felt excluded, Amber realized. She hadn't thought for a second he'd be jealous. She had been certain he'd presume it was all for him.

"Luca, you can't be serious?" Natalia said as she came close to him, and sat beside him, moving her lower limbs atop him. She gently moved her hand across his cheek, and moved her other hand beneath her shirt. Natalia was skilled in the art of placation. She breathed down his neck and held his back—held him close. She whispered something in his ear so Amber couldn't hear. She felt his dick pulse and harden, his body hugged her even though he didn't move his arms around her.

"Amber, let's head out," Natalia said as she mechanically reclothed herself.

Amber had the back seat of the car all to herself, so she sat like a man on a train: legs spread wide. She watched the woods and the picnic area, the small houses, and the road that led to town. She smiled when she saw the vineyard. She didn't want to think about waking up so early tomorrow and working. She pulled out her phone to check the time: 11:38PM. It felt later. She craned her neck and smushed her face onto the window and looked up into the sky to admire the twinkling lights like the city kid she was, in the countryside for the first time in a long time.

Natalia said, "The moon is beautiful tonight."

When Amber looked up, she saw a hole in the sky.

Before she could worry about filling the post-coital car-ride silence, the dogs' barks filled the airwaves. Luca whisper-screamed, "Basta!! Basta," as he pulled the car into the driveway of the Podere.

"Do you think your parents are still up?" Amber asked, finally confirming she could still expel words in her very own voice.

"I dunno, probably in bed watching a movie or something," Luca said.

When they entered the house, however, Marco and Alessandra were not in their room. They were rushing about the house, frantic. Packing things up and making phone calls.

"Tutto bene?" Luca asked.

"Bene sei a casa. Prendi le tue cose. Vestiti, tutto ciò di cui hai bisogno. Stiamo guidando a Bologna il più presto possibile, la nonna Maria è in ospedale," Amber looked to Natalia, concerned and confused. Alessandra continued in English to the girls, "You'll be okay to watch over the house, yes? Amber, I apologize, I know you've just arrived."

"No, no, it's fine. We'll be fine," Amber said.

"Starà bene? Maria, intendo." Natalia asked, and when Alessandra couldn't answer, she asked instead, "What can we do to help?"

"Get some rest. You know where the dog food is and such, the fridge is pretty full. If you need, just go eat at the Trattoria in town. We will pay you back for anything—"

"We'll figure it all out, don't worry. That's for tomorrow," Natalia said.

Amber felt obliged to say *something*, so she mustered up a feeble,

"Let us know if we can do anything. I'm so sorry."

Alessandra smiled and hugged both girls. "I'm so glad you're both here. I don't know what we would be doing. It would be much, much harder. You know this?"

Amber nodded, a pit forming in the center of her body—but no, it wasn't dread compacting, marinating in the pit of her stomach. No, it was a *pit*. A coarse veiny fruit center from which all her base and other instincts and desires derived. Her flesh felt pointless, as her pit was ready to turn her bitter.

She had not kept food or drink down in days. The adults were leaving town. Fleeing their own home, as she had done just days before. But Marco and Alessandra and Luca, well, they had to leave. Amber had felt compelled to jet off and evade her problems. She flitted off to Italy and did not a day's work on a vineyard before slutting it up with the other farmhand and the vineyard owners' son. They weren't leaving because of Charlie. They were leaving because of impending death. God, Amber felt so claustrophobic she couldn't—

She could breathe. She felt for her pulse on her neck.

She was a whore. Charlie was right, and even though she didn't want it. Didn't want him.

She had jerked off thinking of waking up to a dick in her cunt before. Maybe she wanted to be wanted? To be taken? Or even the trauma that came with it? Was she milking this all for more than it was? Was it really that bad? They were friends, after all, back then. She could have said no; she could have stopped him. Maybe it was just bad sex, after all. Just sex gone wrong or prom gone awry. She closed her eyes.

And she felt his hand on her head, pushing her down, and she scrunched up her face. She didn't feel she could have said no. Maybe she wasn't a whore. Just weak. Or maybe she was what her birth certificate claimed: a female. A female body constructed from the rib of Adam. Her body a part of his, indebted to him, made for him and his pleasure alone. Maybe she was less than him, less than human. She was a lady's foot on display in the locker. Which locker? She wasn't a foot. Her phone was locked. Something was afoot. No, her phone was dead. Was there a difference? In sixth grade her friend Arianne was obsessed with calling herself a "female" because "Fe is *iron,* so I am an iron-male, which means I'm Iron Man!" Simple math. All women were the singular Iron Man. Amber didn't want to be Iron Man. She didn't want to be some Man. She didn't want to be anything. She wasn't a lady or a woman, a man, or even a girl. She was a collection of holes and water. Humanbits, flesh, muscles, skin, blood, calories amassed into the mass that made her. Maybe she should go to mass. She should've gone to the Vatican. She couldn't escape the cage of her own flesh. She had fled New York. She was barely online. He haunted her mind.

At the other Podere, she had liked when the dick was in her asshole because she liked feeling like the dirty slut—craved the validation of her greatest fears. She liked feeling like she was nothing but holes. Her pores, wide open, expelling sweat. Her cunthole, asshole, mouthhole all used up—filled by space she couldn't herself fill, would never let herself take up.

She liked imagining somehow one of those boys filmed them all having sex back there. That he'd upload it and ruin her life for her. So she couldn't ruin it for herself.

She would make so much jizz with her moving image. Think of all the people who'd cum looking at her holding hands with Natalia.

Natalia.

Natalia was looking at her, bags under her eyes. When did she get so tired? Had she slept last night? Was she okay? Her nose was so perfect. She hoped no one had ever told her its tip protruded too much. It was a perfect button nose, she wanted to kiss it. No, she wanted to bite it.

"Are you okay?" Natalia asked.

"Did they leave?" Amber said.

"Amber, you said goodbye to them," Natalia said.

"I feel terrible," Amber said.

"You should eat. You're starving yourself," Natalia said.

Amber nodded.

"Have an apricot, and I will make you something good," Natalia said.

"I'm afraid I did this to myself," Amber said.

"What?" Natalia said.

"I think the world is—I feel like—you know how on the show they said rumination can start with a virus?" Amber said.

"Yes, or by trauma or many other things," Natalia said.

"What if I'm—."

"Amber. The world is on fire. Up is down and down is up. None of this is your fault. We are both so tired, and have had a crazy day."

The house felt haunted in its abandonment. Amber and Natalia sat on their respective dinnertime stools as Natalia spooned out the remnants of the dulce de leche gelato straight from the pint.

"This is so good, I feel bad."

"It's not your fault I can't eat."

"Maybe it's not the rumination. Maybe it's just your digestion."

"I just—when we were watching that show, like, I just felt it in my bones, you know? I know I have it even if I don't obviously officially know I do."

"When I was anorexic and knew if I kept it up my family would find out because I would have to be hospitalized, I would go into the bathroom with a packet of string cheese and would look myself in the eyes and say to myself 'You are fucking anorexic,' until I cried and ate the whole piece of cheese," Natalia said.

"Whoa."

"I know what it feels like to know what's happening to your body, even if you feel responsible, and to feel like you can't do anything about it."

"How'd you start eating again?" Amber asked.

"Slowly," Natalia said as she got up from the stool and walked to the sink to rinse out the gelato carton. She threw it into the recycling.

"When I was in Rome I, like, debated whether I should spend all my time there to see the Vatican and I didn't go," Amber said, unsure why exactly.

"Do you feel guilty?" Natalia said.

"I'm not Catholic, but what if I'm wrong?" Amber said.

"Do you think you're being punished?" Natalia said.

"Not really," Amber said.

"You don't believe in God?" Natalia said.

"I believe in wholeness?" Amber said.

"Holiness?" Amber asked.

"No, more like, I think I believe everything in the universe is one great, big whole— and that Whole could be what we refer to as God? Like collectively, we all make up God, or parts of it, them, whatever. Like, yeah, like I feel like—I think we are all just a bunch of holes who together make up one Whole," Amber said.

"Wholes who make up a whole? I don't understand."

"No, no—holes. Like, everyone has at least an anus? A mouth? We all have holes. We are all just holes. You know?"

Natalia said, "Interesting."

"And together we're a bunch of holes. Who make up on big collection."

"Of holes. One Whole hole. I see. Hm—."

"It's stupid."

Natalia said, "It's not stupid."

"Maybe not, but I feel stupid."

"Why's that?"

"Did you know what was going to happen earlier?"

"That they would leave for Bologna? Of course not."

"No. The other thing."

"Oh. Not particularly," Natalia said before adding, "But I was glad when it did."

"I felt like I was my holes. I think that is our base, human state."

Natalia said nothing.

"What are you?"

"I'm German and Italian."

"I get it. You're fascist," Amber breathed in and out four times before saying, "I'm kidding. I'm Jewish. I don't know why I said that. I wanna bite your lip."

"I think you're right," Natalia said, "I think we're all just holes who want to be filled in some way or another, by other holes in the universe. So together, when we work, our holes fill other holes, and that's how we, individually, can become Whole."

Once she finished, the talking stopped, and they kissed like they were licking ice cream from the cone, or cats lapping milk. Gently—until they got a taste of the other.

"You taste like caramel," Amber said.

"Maybe my spit will feed you," Natalia said.

"That's disgusting."

"I know."

"I love it."

"Me too."

"When I was little—never mind."

"What?"

"No, it's so embarrassing."

"Now you have to tell me."

"Fine. When I was little, I studied penguins? And became, like, obsessed with them. All my friends' parents were getting divorced, and I think I liked the idea of people mating for life. It's stupid, but it just felt secure?"

Natalia said, "No, I agree. Having one person is a beautiful theory," then shook her head, before she said, "It's beautiful in theory. It reminds me of Symposium, the fourth speech. The one myth where people used to be conjoined: two in one. But the Gods saw that as a threat? So, Zeus cut us all in half."

"I've never read *Symposium*," Amber said.

"You should. It has lots of theories. Of love and, you know, everything."

"Interesting—. Anyway, yeah, I dunno. I guess because of that, the mating, I got super into everything about penguins. But not just, like, their mating patterns."

"Okay?" Natalia acknowledged, unsure where exactly this was going.

"It's so stupid. I don't even know why I'm telling you this."

"Amber, you can tell me. I'm not gonna judge you."

"You barely know me."

"Don't lie."

"Sorry."

"Tell me about the penguins."

"Their mothers eat the food for their babies. Like they consume it, and regurgitate it back for them?"

"Okay?"

"I dunno. I've been thinking about it a lot."

"Amber? Do you want me to feed you?"

Amber rolled her eyes and kissed Natalia, licking the roof of her mouth with her tongue, then scraping Natalia's tongue with her teeth, until she reached her lips: she bit down, then she breathed, "I'm okay."

"You sure you don't want to eat?" Natalia said.

"I should probably try again to eat something, but I hate tasting like my own vomit," Amber stood, but Natalia gestured for her to stay seated.

"What are you in the mood for?"

"Something simple, I think. Maybe toast or if there's pasta leftover," Amber said.

"I'll make fresh pasta," Natalia said.

"Are you sure?? I'm, like, fully capable of using the microwave or toaster—-whatever," Amber said.

"I'll make fresh pasta. Without the sauce. The acid has to be tough coming back up, no?" Natalia said as she opened the cupboard and took stock of the boxes of pasta, asking Amber, "Spaghetti or penne?"

"Spaghetti maybe? That could be nice."

Natalia took the box and placed it on the counter. From the fridge she grabbed parmesan and fresh peas, which were tucked away in a drawer reserved for produce. She opened another compartment and found pancetta. From the center of the kitchen island, she acquired an onion and two cloves of garlic. She came back for a third.

She heated oil in a saucepan, "You know you always have to have oil on the pan before you heat the stove, yes?" Natalia asked.

"I normally do, I think," Amber said.

"You do that so it doesn't heat up the pan, and get all the pan particles into your food. Instead, it just heats the oil, preparing it for whatever you're cooking," Natalia said.

"Do you like to cook?" Amber asked.

"My mother taught me what her mother taught her. Men get surnames and women get recipes," Natalia said.

"Do you actually believe that?" Amber said.

Natalia took off the cling wrap covering the package of pancetta, and shook all its contents into the pan. Oil splattered as the cured pork belly sizzled. "No, of course not. But that's how it is. She wasn't around, and yet she made the time to teach me to cook."

Amber nodded, and her mind traveled from her head and her heart back to her stomach. Perhaps she had developed, or would develop, an ulcer from this. Stomach acids gnawing away at her digestive tract, her body eating away at her own body because it couldn't manage to consume anything else at all. Her antibodies hadn't protected her from some virus or stressor, whatever. Her body had become anti-body. Her stomach felt large and imposing, bloated like a body after days of decomposition. Gasses in the abdomen, foam from the mouth. Her body was decomposing, bloating itself alive.

"My grandfather was a butcher, you know." Natalia said.

Amber made some interested noise so she knew she was listening and cared.

"When I was fifteen, he had my brother harvest a pig, and then I had to help my grandmother cure the carcass."

"Jesus, that's the most insane form of family bonding. Though, I guess my grandpa made me re-pot his bonsai trees with him when we visited. Did you live near your grandparents?"

"They were in Liguria," Natalia said.

"How do you even cure a dead animal?" Amber asked.

"We didn't heal it. Just made it last. That's how you say it in English, right? To cure," Natalia said.

"Yeah, sorry. How do you cure meat? With salt?" Amber said.

"We used—hmmm I don't know how to say it," Natalia opened her phone and searched Google translate before continuing on to say, "mustard seeds, coriander, nutmeg, black pepper, fennel, star anise, and juniper berries. Ground them up with a—not mortar—."

"Pestle?"

"Yes, and then my grandma made the curing salt by mixing salt and the, um, nitrite, and spread it onto a layer of parchment paper which lined sheet pan. She let me sprinkle the seasonings over the salt before we moved the pig's belly onto the pan," Natalia said.

Amber imagined fatty layers of white mixed in with light layers of millennial pink-colored pork.

"That's the day I learned how to zest an orange," Natalia said.

"That's cool, I guess."

"I would've figured that much out at some point."

"Why'd you need to zest an orange?"

"So, we could massage it into the flesh and turn the layer of white fat orange. My grandma taught me that for the best pancetta, you're supposed to get the essence under its skin."

Amber gained eighteen pounds after everything happened last semester. She would eat, and be full, but her stomach still craved something, so she'd get seconds, thirds. Have dessert. She gained space, and ripped through pants. She was still not heavy, just thicker. Skinny thicc. She had been eating just fine, eating and eating, and calming her nerves with food.

The once-white lining of fat in the diced pancetta crisped and browned in the oil on the pan in front of them. The pink meat turned bloodied maroon.

Amber was fine. She was fine and then she wasn't fine. But she had been fine in her not-fine-ness, in her rabid consumption to fill her soul: a black hole.

"I wish you could cure me," Amber said.

"Huh?"

"It's supposed to keep things from spoiling, right?"

"Sure, but the things have to be dead. It only keeps them good for the living."

"Can you tell me more?"

"More about what?"

"About your grandma."

"Yeah, I mean, she doesn't do much but cook and work and sleep, and like talk about me finding a husband and my mom being a wife," Natalia said.

"Oh," Amber said.

"But the rest of the pancetta story is kind of—I dunno. So, you have to cover the belly in curing salt completely and then my grandma was like, "this will teach you patience." Oh, also, yeah, so they kind of made my brother kill the pig because he was a boy. And they made me cure the meat because my grandma thought— well she explained it to me by saying that she and grandpa both take pride and pleasure in their work, and it makes them frugal and patient. And so, we had done all the work, and like what felt like forever but I think was only like a week went by, and my grandma came up to me and was all dramatic, and was like—it's time! And they we rinsed and rolled it and cleaned it and tied it in like one of those little cheesecloth things, and I was ready to try it. Like, we had done the work and waited and done more work, you know?" Natalia said.

"Yeah, totally," Amber said.

"And my grandma was like—still no," Natalia said.

"No!!"

"Which I thought was bullshit, clearly. My brother got to put a bullet through its brain—immediate gratification. He had a task and completed it. I told her I didn't want to cure the pig. And my grandma—I'd never seen her like this—she turned so quiet and solemn and I felt like I had just betrayed her, which also made me mad. I thought I was being a feminist sort of, not betraying my grandmother, you know?"

"So, what happened?" Amber asked.

"Nothing for months. My grandma continued curing whatever my grandpa killed, and I mostly forgot about it. And I just like drank gross blue drinks at high school parties and did other people's homework for money," Natalia said.

"You didn't."

"No, yeah, I did. And then one day my grandma woke me up at 5AM and I was pissed because I had only gone to sleep hours before—but that's when she began her work every day. And she took me with her and she showed me different ways to cut it up. You know, how to slice the cured flesh that we had prepared together. She said it was mine to finish. She just left me down there with this huge pork belly," Natalia said.

Amber thought of the lining of fat around her stomach. She used to be able to see an outline of her abs, but she had grown herself a muffin top.

"What did you do with it?" Amber asked.

Natalia turned down the heat on the pancetta. She chopped an onion, and minced the garlic, before mixing it in with the diced, cured pork belly. She said, "I ate the whole thing."

Amber breathed in for five counts, out for ten. Once. Twice. Three times. To force herself back to the present moment. "You said you were anorexic."

Natalia sighed as she gently mixed the contents of the pan. The water in the pot began to bubble, boiling. She took off the lid, and her face was shrouded with steam as she said, "You know how Alessandra serves the boys so much more food than us?"

"Yeah," Amber said.

Natalia took all the spaghetti from its box, and held it in her hands, breaking it all in half over the water. "Can you set a timer for eight minutes?" Amber did, and Natalia continued mixing the onions. She added in the cheese and the peas, then said, "Growing up with a brother—. I cared a lot about fairness, so if he ate something, I had to eat it, too. But then I got older, and I began to help out with cooking. So, I would take a taste, try this or that, and also have a full meal, seconds and desserts."

Amber blushed.

"You understand," Natalia said.

Amber smiled; she did.

Natalia continued, "I ate a lot, but I was skinny, so no one cared. But then I got a boyfriend, and he'd make comments. I didn't let them get to me; I thought he was being an asshole, actually, so I dumped him and got a new boyfriend. But by then, I was older and my—I don't know the word in English. Stoffwechsel? Metabolismo?"

"Oh, metabolism," Amber said.

"Yes, my metabolism had slowed down, and so I was eating just the same, but now gaining some weight. And he didn't say it was why he broke up with me. But he broke up with me, and people were also making comments about my body, and I did the math. I wanted to be desirable, so I taught myself to desire nothing," Natalia said.

"How did you—?"

"Get better?" Natalia asked.

"Yeah," Amber said.

"I wanted to feel satisfied and not just satisfy someone else," Natalia said.

"You just woke up one day and realized that?" Amber said.

"I told you already. I cured a pig and ate its belly. It was my pancetta. She said I could do whatever I wanted with it, and you must understand, I hadn't eaten more than just one piece of cheese or a slice of bread every day—coffee and cigarettes were what made me feel full. If I put milk in coffee, that was my meal, you understand? I was so hungry—. You see, before this, eating felt violent. Life sustaining my life meant mass death of lettuce, of cows, of blueberries, salmon, apricots, and grapes. But I ate the whole belly. Its body fed me—was survived by me. I saw my brother killing it with every bite I took. I consumed our energy and effort. Eating it became beautiful and not so traumatizing. Life sustaining life. It's like some sort of immortality. Unity. A lineage of existence, but not ancestral," Natalia said.

"Am I dying?" Amber asked.

"But I am, too," Natalia said.

"Why aren't we all screaming? If life is just slow death," Amber said.

Natalia said, "I don't know."

After a long moment of contemplation, Amber said, "If I die, I want you to cure me," as her eyes brimmed with tears and her phone alarm beeped and buzzed, breaking the spell.

Natalia returned to the stove to taste test un spaghetto. The verdict: perfectly al dente. She strained the water from the pasta, keeping only a few spoonfuls of pasta water to add to the pan. She poured the pasta in with the onions, which were turning jammy and brown. She mixed the noodles into the forming sauce, then added more cheese.

"It smells so good," Amber said.

Natalia smiled, and turned off the heat. She grabbed a bowl from the countertop and filled it to its brim, perfectly selecting each ounce of the portion. Taking care, ensuring the noodle-to-pancetta-to-peas-to-cheese-to-garlic-to-onions ratio was perfetto.

"You're not having any?" Amber asked.

Natalia rolled her eyes, and picked up a fork. She slurped up the deliciously presented noodles on her own, not offering any to Amber.

"Can I have a bite?" Amber said.

"Patience, sweet penguin," Natalia smiled, mid-chew.

"I'm literally starving, like legitimately."

"Drink some water. You'll probably dehydrate before you starve," which Amber realized was true, so she finished her glass and poured herself some more. Natalia then said, "Do you remember when splooshing was a big thing?"

"Splooshing?" Amber said.

"That cake-sitting fetish thing? Where people would sit, totally naked, on cakes and fancy, messy sweets and that was like, what was hot," Natalia said.

"Oh, like Vice or someplace did some story on it that went viral," Amber said.

"Yeah," Natalia said.

"Yeah, I vaguely remember that. It makes sense. Like, people love consumption but wanna be skinny. So, like, the peak of excess, of consumer culture, is buying and using without really consuming," Amber said.

"I kinda thought it was hot. Food as sex object."

"No, yeah. I mean, I don't— disagree. I guess."

"For a while, I had this fantasy—." Natalia stopped talking, to take a bite. She carefully twirled the noodles onto her fork, nudging bits of pancetta and a few peas onto the tip of the utensil, encouraging them with the tips of the fork's tines. She chewed, and Amber watched her neck move with each bite. She swallowed.

"What was your fantasy?" Amber said, but she felt like she was watching from the ceiling of the room. She felt like the white paint on the kitchen's ceiling looking down at them, purified and naive. Empty, like a canvas waiting to be filled and spoiled. Rotten. An un-scraped tongue.

"I wanted to consume the whole wide world. But I wanted someone to force me to do it, so I could not be responsible. You know? If I got fat or unattractive, I wanted to because someone had forced me to eat. I mostly dreamed of this when things were really bad, when I wasn't eating at all really and I would get lightheaded and start daydreaming because I was so close to fainting. I imagined— actually, I imagined my calculus teacher taking me out for currywurst and forcing me to eat the whole sausage.— And in my mind, it wasn't a good wurst, you know? It was like—you could tell it was fried. It was oily, and the casing was thick. It was ugly, and the curry was—it wasn't, I don't know, it was too sweet? And the chips, or, how do you say? Fries. They were so limp and—and soggy, and tasted of, yeah, of oil and fat. I felt like I was being forced into eating fat. And he was making me eat this sausage, and I kept telling him that I didn't want to eat the wurst, but he said I must, or otherwise I would die. Or maybe he didn't say that exactly, maybe that's just how I felt. You know how that happens, in dreams. You don't know what's real, what's not. It all melds and shifts and changes, keeps becoming a new version of itself every time you remember," Natalia became solemn as she took another bite and continued, "Come here," as she chewed the food into a happy pulp, wordlessly deciding the pancetta had been prepared lovingly.

Amber leaned in to meet Natalia, who kissed her—mouth open, no tongue, with a food offering. Amber's gut reaction was to laugh and pull away, embarrassed. But Natalia held her firmly as she shared the contents of her mouth with Amber. Amber tensed up at first, but was able to relax and swallow.

She tasted Natalia's saliva mixed in with the pasta, which made it taste slightly off, or spoiled. Amber cleared her throat as a sort of sound check to make sure she could still make noise before she croaked out, "Sometimes I wonder if it matters what's real and what's imagined. They both have impact," Amber said.

"Yeah, I don't know if it was a dream though. I can't remember. It may have been a nightmare then. I don't remember how I felt," Natalia said.

Amber's throat tensed and her mind started screaming for her to move, but her body didn't want to leave the present moment. She wanted the pre-chewed food to nourish her back to health. She wanted Natalia's spit enzymes to break down the pasta so she didn't have to break down herself.

She got up and ran to the compost. It was almost full. It smelled of pits and eggshells. If she hadn't already the desire to upchuck, the smell alone would have done it. Watery, cream-colored sludge escaped her mouth. She wiped her face clean with the back of her hand before she cleaned herself off properly in the sink.

"Sorry," Amber said, as she ran the water.

"It's okay. I have another idea," Natalia said.

"Gandhi survived a 21-day hunger strike. I'm not even at a week yet," Amber said.

"We still have time to figure this out, you mean?" Natalia said.

"Have you been checking Instagram?" Amber asked.

"What?" Natalia said.

"Alessandra said not to use up the WiFi, so I haven't been checking social media really," Amber said.

"Amber, yes, I've been checking social media. It's slow as hell, but—." Natalia shoveled in bite after bite of noodles and pork and peas and cheese.

Natalia held the breath in her mouth and swallowed some spit before releasing a large belch. She took a breath. Then made herself burp again. And again, and again, and again. It was smaller each she forced air up and out of her. Air from her insides, rejoined with the atmosphere.

Amber took a deep breath in, trying to suck in any air particles from Natalia's innards, so they could meld with her own insides.

"Are you trying to smell my burps?" Natalia asked.

Amber shook her head. "I'm trying to eat the air you've breathed and rejected. And ejected, I guess, too."

Natalia considered this, and then cautiously asked, "Do you really want me to cure you if you die?"

Amber's look turned tender; she nodded.

Natalia's face lost its color, and she said with such vigor, "Come here." Her stomach tensed, like she'd been punched straight in the gut.

Amber rushed to her side and asked, "Are you alright?"

"Just kiss me now, okay??"

Their mouths collided—lips on lips, tongues on tongues—something warm and chunky hit the tip of Amber's tongue. It tasted acidic and soft, like something a baby would eat. Upon realizing, she bit down on Natalia's tongue, and scraped the remnants of the mushy substance from her mouth, into her own. She swallowed, then connected mouths, again. More vomit awaited her. A pea unchewed, she swallowed. She suckled Natalia's mouth until her spit had begun tasting sweet again, the vomit stopped, and she was coughing. Amber clutched her shoulder, and patted her back, to make sure she was okay. Natalia regained her composure. Amber lost hers. She swallowed nutrients, then hurried to the compost, thinking pragmatically during this time of unique crisis. She barfed up Natalia's regurgitate. Tears streamed from her eyes while Natalia's pre-digested food left her body.

Natalia came to her side, and held her. "Can we go sleep now?"

Amber nodded, then said, "For a moment, we were both flour, water, salt, peas, butter, and pancetta."

Natalia tightened their embrace, and whispered into her ear, "Don't forget the garlic, sweet penguin."

"Do you remember anything else?" Amber said," About the pig?"

Natalia shrugged and said "His mother outlived him, but his life was okay, even nice."

"That's all??"

"He liked this one spot of grassless dirt. He liked licking the dirt. Made him feel full. Remember when grass-flavored Jelly Bellies were a thing?"

Amber did remember. She liked them, even.

Eventually the girls ran out of pig pi I chatter hatter and an a scurried curried up the stairs to their heir bathrooms, where they brushed rushed their teeth and tried to clean lean their mouths from that enamel-wearing, drunken, rancid taste of spit pit it i and bile.

"If you leave me, I think I'll die," Amber said.

"Don't say that," Natalia said.

"But it's the truth," Amber said.

"Well, then I won't leave you," Natalia said.

They fell asleep in Natalia's bed, both becoming dead weight on the other. Cutting off circulation in some limb or another: Amber's arm, Natalia's leg. Or was it Natalia's arm and Amber's leg? Neither knew, and they couldn't keep track. Together, their heir breath escaped, their hearts heart hear beat, their lungs breathed.

Love is a serious mental disease.

—according to brainyquote.com, Plato

It had only been three days since the family had left their land. Since then, Amber and Natalia began to barely notice the countryside filled with its dry, thirsty land, and budding vineyards—even the grapes forming under overturned vines and the hairy spiders and their endless webs seemed to have lost their luster. Marco had told them to just make sure everything was combed and weeded by the time they returned—though they did not yet know when that might be.

Amber and Natalia decided to do their fieldwork at odd, sunless hours so they could unwind and chill during normal times. They worked from five or six till ten or eleven in the morning. Natalia did the more rigorous work. She squatted and crawled down in the dirt, searching for the roots of weeds to rip them up and cut their flowers from their stalks. Amber kept on with the combing. Natalia had convinced Amber by saying she must conserve her caloric-deficit contributing actions for all the crazy sex they would inevitably continue to have. Amber had discovered that even too much spit and discharge can trigger her gag reflex. She hoped this gag reflex wouldn't give her acid reflux.

But after she and Natalia worked until their minds went numb and their fingers felt dull with dirt, they showered each other with kisses and soap and water, then lay naked in the grass, more for the aesthetic than out of comfort. Dried mud and blades of grass stuck to their bums and stained their backs, but they pretended to enjoy even the company of bugs and the flies as they focused attention on their touching limbs and playing footsie while they played the podcast *Eating Alone in My Car* from Natalia's portable speaker.

The episode was entitled "hot pockets" but Melissa Broder barely discussed the bready-but-crumby layer of crust and its scalding, squirting filling. Melissa talked instead about how she wanted to occupy the state of nothingness. And how she doesn't drink water and eats like shit and loves the sun, so she's perpetually-dehydrated. She eats so much Splenda in a day she'll surely never be well-hydrated, but she can't bring herself to drink water. She also talked about her shopping bulimia, and how buying and returning objects "fills you up until it doesn't and then everything is disgusting."

Amber and Natalia were quiet as they listened, for it felt like she had heard their thoughts and was answering them in podcast form. Their quiet consideration of her meandering rambling became an anxious meditation, a prayer? A prayer to Melissa. Perhaps this was Amber's Vatican. Melissa: her pope, diva, idol. Natalia: a fellow worshipper.

The episode ended and *Slate Money* blasted without any moment of silence. Natalia pressed pause, and said, "I want to read something wonderful."

Amber nodded feeling pressured suddenly, to consume content. To look literate. Not allow herself to sit around and bask in Natalia's presence, drink in her essence. She remembered her parents and Emma, and school. She had been ignoring her phone. Blocking out her real life from her mind. The whole world and the worldwide web flooded back into her brain's consciousness. She had forgotten for a moment just how—incomplete she was.

How dare she feel satisfied?

"Do you have a book you want to read?" Amber said as she realized she had taken Natalia's affection for granted. She had forgotten that the clout of being an American at some known university had given her undeserved credit. She forgot she had to prove she was everything she feared she wasn't. She felt guilty for not having read or watched any of the books and movies she'd brought and downloaded for the trip. Why was she so incapable of participating in society as a functional human person? What had she done? She had gone off to college and instead of making the friends she was supposed to cling onto for life, she repelled them. She existed in ways that led to her isolation. And when she felt so alone in her own city, she fled. To do what? Clear her head? Her mind was filled with too many holes to ever stop top to o to top stop. STOP.

"Reading to each other could be hot. I've been meaning to start Anna Karenina," Natalia said.

"That'd take like forever, though," Amber said. Her insides felt shaky and unhinged.

"You don't like this idea?" Natalia said.

Amber loved the idea—she wanted nothing more than to sit outside in this field with Natalia and read to each other and drink wine and pretend to enjoy eating the apricots she couldn't stomach, not that she could stomach anything at this point. And wasn't that the crux of it all. She knew this beautiful moment was as precarious as the spiderwebs they broke, which clung to the vines as they waited to be torn from being.

"Nat?" Amber said.

To which Natalia replied, "Yes, my dear Ambrosia."

"What if this is it?"

"Don't be silly," Natalia said.

"I think I should call my parents," Amber said, unable to explain more than that her mind was spasming— glitching. She couldn't say how she felt and she knew that. "I've been weak all week." Wee we E. She's he's he e been bee be e week wee we e. "I can't think." I can't can an a think thin. "I think the hunger broke my mind, or my mind's been broken."

"Amber, you're scaring me."

"I'm scaring me," Amber said. "You know how it's the wrinkles on your brain that are like what make us smart?"

"I think so," Natalia said.

"It feels like my mind is operating in the space between the wrinkles. Like, I can't think. Or like I am forced to think the way I think. Like with the subtitles— I'm being forced to think the way I think thin. Like, I feel like I'm dubbing over myself," Amber said.

"You mean performing?" Natalia said.

"I am not okay," Amber said. "I feel like I'm dying and I'm not ready for this."

"Let's go to the hospital."

"They'll have no clue what to do."

"Who cares? You won't starve."

Laughter spilled from Amber's lips.

"What?"

"I don't want to go to."

"What?" Natalia said.

Amber shook her head and pushed herself on top of Natalia.

"What are you saying?? You aren't okay. I think we should get help."

"I'm just delirious," Amber said as she drew Natalia's hands back, above her head—drove them deep into the dirt and held them down as she kissed Natalia's neck. Natalia's breath became shallow. She stopped relenting and started to beg. Amber released her hold on Natalia's hands, and kissed her clavicle, then her breasts—she suckled until Natalia made some salacious sound.

Amber whispered in Natalia's ear, "I'm okay now. I love you." She licked Natalia's ear, breathed into it—the ear hairs that gave her direction prickled—Amber bit down, pulling on her earlobe. Then slapped her cheek rosy.

Natalia grabbed Amber's head in her hands, Amber's hair got stuck in their mouths, so they had to spit her hair out before they ate each other's mouths out—teeth scraping tongues, biting lips. Teeth on teeth. Spit on spit. No pit in her stomach, only dirty tongues and filthier minds.

"I just need your spit to survive," Amber said.

Natalia moved Amber onto the dirt, and kissed her wetly on the cheek before quietly saying, "I need you to be okay. Okay?" She continued down Amber's body, and ate her out like the juiciest fucking apricot. Amber gasped and pulled Natalia's hair and wanted to cry as she said, "I'm—," but couldn't finish saying the words, because she was cumming too hard.

She she he e she's coming coming.

e. e. cummings' coming.

She was coming.

She wa—

Cum cum cum cum cum cum um um um—

"Amber, you look—grey?? Are you okay? Let's stop. Do you want orange juice???"

Amber blacked out.

Her body was sore and spent. Her eyes felt like they were sinking into the ground. There were storm clouds above. Where was Natalia? She should call her mother. The clouds were so beautiful: Rainy Day on Quiet Grey on Cool Grey on Storming Ahead on Mother of Pearl on Titanium on Steel My Heart on Glacier Grey on Bleached Coral on Lilac Grey on blankness. On White. Off-White. Crushing blankness. White as a ghost. Light rays fighting through. Cannoli Cream. Hint of Sunshine. Eggshell.

She'd been stepping on eggshells, trying not to offend. Obsessing alone at night. Going over everything that happened—was she the one being crazy? Emma said no. Emma had been there, practically. For most of it, anyway. Emma knew. Emma saw. She agreed. Amber wasn't crazy. They walked on eggshells together. Amber didn't want things to be weird or strange. They were all friends. It could all be normal still. She liked having a big group of friends. She imagined the reunions they would have someday. One night couldn't ruin that. The night after she blacked out in her dorm room all alone. She called her mother and cried. Her mother didn't know she was blacked out. She woke up completely covered by her sheets and pillows. She could have suffocated. She woke up to her mother knocking on her door asking if she was okay. She was suffocating. She couldn't stop apologizing. Her mother had come to New Jersey.

When she stopped walking on eggshells, he started to yell at her in his eggshell-colored room. She wanted to break him. Use him. Yolk him. Steal his egg. White. Whit. Walt Whitman said, "Oxen that rattle the yoke and chain or halt in the leafy shade, what is that you express in your eyes? It seems to me more than all the print I have read in my life." What the fuck did yoke mean anyway? Where did Natalia go? Where did Natalia go??? Did Natalia go?

"Natalia??!!!" Amber called out.

The trees and the grass and the vines swayed in response.

Amber rolled on her side, and lifted herself up. Her weight felt hollow. Her vision, purple. She felt the turning of the planet. The clouds were moving so quickly. She moved hair from her face. She was sweating profusely. No, those were tears. Tear ear. Her ears were ringing. She looked at her finger. She'd never get married.

Where was Natalia? There was no one, just land.

"NATALIA?!"

Nothing. Natalia must've gone inside and left her to rest.

"Natalia," she said with her hands coiled around her mouth, "NA-TALIAAAAA!!!!!" Her hands vibrated like they were made of heat or of light.

The vineyard: no Natalia. The garden: no Natalia.

The house: no signs of life. Her stomach was fermenting its own acids. She wondered if she could whine her way to wine made from her own stomach acids. Which was the dream? Everything before, or this now? Natalia existed.

Amber looked down at her body. Her skin was blotchy and bloated and lumpy. So full on nothing. She looked at the floor. Her feet were unshoed. Her feet were on tiles now, cool and blue slate. She didn't know where she'd left her shoes. She didn't have a locker and she wasn't a woman. She wasn't a female a woman a lady. She wasn't he wasn't she was he was as a an iron man a female emale e-mail. Amber thought it'd be smart to check her emails. Where was Natalia?

"Natalia?" She said he said aid id I— "Natalia?????????????" She said as she opened her phone and WhatsApp'd Natalia:

Natalia??????????????

She was only yet in the foyer, but felt the whole building in her body. She became the building—they were both empty together. Even the dogs must've been outside. She was alone lone one on o she was so alone and she felt it in her tit or in her heart hear ear she could hear a ringing in her ear. She looked down. Her phone in her hand was ringing. It was her mother.

"Mom?"

"Honey, hi—let me grab your father," her mother said.

"Wait, no. Sorry—"

"What's up? Amber, you sound—"

"How do I sound?"

"You're cutting out—" Amber's mom said.

"You started saying that I sound—??"

"Are you okay? Do you like the family? Are they feeding you?"

"Um. I don't know. Mom, I don't want you to worry," Amber said.

To which her mother immediately replied, "Should I be worried? Are you okay?"

"I think I need to come home," Amber said.

"Why? Are you okay??"

"I'm," Amber started as her voice caught in her throat. "There's this thing—there's this place—."

"You're worrying me, honey, just say whatever it is. It'll be okay," Amber's mom said.

"Sorry, I'm fine. I love you. I'm just. I have a crush," Amber said.

"That's great news—" Her mother said, just before the call cut out.

Amber was abandoned again. She stumbled forward as she checked WhatsApp: nothing new. No messages. She dialed Natalia's number: no answer.

Fuck.

She craved a dopamine hit; opened Twitter:

@drappleistheog: everclear on tap for our wounds

@drappleistheog: sloths are real

@iconiqueboibish: I GET IT YOU'RE GAY SO AM I BUT IM NOT BLASTING MYSTERY OF LOVE AT 5AM

@edithwhoreton: sumer is icumen in on repeat

At 7:06, a text from Emma popped up:

 Can you check Allie's twitter for me

 She blocked me

         I don't follow her is she private

         She might've blocked me too but I'll check

 should be public

 I just don't wanna google bc

 I will keep googling it

 Sorry

 Ik I'm being annoying

         Ur so fine please we've all

Amber opened Twitter and read:

@lacroixifixion: what r u supposed to do with ur hands??

 @iconiqueboibish: and arms!

Amber searched Allie Panybud'laska. Her bio read: poly pan am cunty verse.

@addiedaddy: im a communist which means im a capitalism who believes u should venmo me ur money

@addiedaddy: costar says I'm spiraling, but I feel great. Is this—. delusion?

@addiedaddy: blocked the toxic out of my life!

@addiedaddy: who can I crash w? Will make u vegan treats as thanks

@addiedaddy: idk what to say I'm a Shane not a bette

She took a screenshot and sent it to Emma before she opened WhatsApp and messaged Natalia:

> Nat — I feel crazy where r u
>
> I feel like I invented you
>
> I'm sorry if I fucked anything up
>
> I'm so worried
>
> I totally blacked out
>
> I wasn't drunk??? Like I don't know
>
> I'm just sorry if I
>
> I didn't mean to
>
> I love you
>
> I hope you know that
>
> Duck
>
> *duck
>
> Fuck
>
> Fuck spellcheck hates me
>
> Anyway
>
> Call me or text or idk but like this is
>
> Killing me

A text from Emma popped up:

> OMG

Amber opened their messages as new texts materialized before her eyes.

Thank you

God I feel like an addict?

I swear I'll get over it

                                        Dude you dated for awhile

                                        You're allowed time to like

                                                        Process

She's so shitty wow

                                                        Yeah dude

                                                             Crazy

                                          Did you kick her out

Kinda

                                                                Like

                                                               Fair

I'm gonna go to yoga think

But I love you

                                                                Ok!

                                                  Love you too

I can't believe she literally said

Blocked the toxic out of my life

After she blocked ME

I—

                                                             Insane

                                                     Like truly

Amber opened Twitter again and kept scrolling, trying to distract her brain and keep herself from spiraling. She didn't even care about the internet anymore. This was practically therapy, she convinced herself. How much could one internet binge cost? She was barely downloading content, only looking at images and text and thinking obsessively over Natalia. She couldn't have ave left eft her. Did id she he really leave?

@edithwhoreton: all I want is to be uglyhot

@edithwhoreton: plato's symposium coming to Starz next fall !!!

@lacroixifixion: came out to my mom as a stand-up comic lol

@edithwhoreton: Grimes looks like that??

@drappleistheog: my cat is trying to drink my coffee

    @edithwhoreton: luv her

        @drappleistheog: I know

She opened the search window and hesitated. She searched for Charlie. His bio read: whiskey & catcher in the rye

@Char1ieB3ar47: working in Memphis has made me an alocoholic

@Char1ieB3ar47: someting's afoot in the new OUATIH trailer

    @Char1ieB3ar47: Quentin tarantino sells socks now too

@Char1ieB3ar47: good improv is worse than bad improv

@Char1ieB3ar47: not even ashamed about how much I loved Spider-man

She searched for Laney, whose bio read: 1% crazy 99% that's rich

@Bluestonelaney: yes im rewatching a simple life what of it

@Bluestonelaney: can u be fired from an unpaid internship

@Bluestonelaney: spring break all summer bb !!!

@Bluestonelaney: whoa literally never been hungover, just always keep drinking stay hydrated kids bops

@Bluestonelaney: lexi hooked up with the bouncer at mcbain I'm — obsessed

Robby's bio was: surviving my dark ages.

@PiuOMenoRobby: whoa haahahaa hahha

@PiuOMenoRobby: buffalo buffalo buffalo buffalo buffalo buffalo buffalo

    @PiuOMenoRobby: buffalo x 7 = 7(buffalo)

                @PiuOMenoRobby: seven buffalo walk into a sentence

                      @PiuOMenoRobby: what happens when a hums major tries to do math

@PiuOMenoRobby: deftly daft

@PiuOMenoRobby: the new york times is a newspaper and also a website

      @PiuOMenoRobby: I like their crossword puzzles

           @PiuOMenoRobby: yes daddy Vladimir im a bot promoting fake news

                                  Emma I went down a hole

                                            I hate them

Nooooo

Charlie's twitter?

Is it bad

I unfollowed

                                                    Idk

                                               It's just

                                       ahhhhhhhhhhh

                                               I feel like

HA

Mood

Honestly such an underrated momenT

A perfect pic

The Starbucks frap

                                               Ik right

She went back to Twitter and continued to scroll through her newsfeed.

@lacroixifixion: you wanna fuck the hot priest, I wanna be the hot priest, we are not the same

@drappleistheog: David Hockney and Elton John are HOT

@edithwhoreton: what about warhol?

@lacroixifixion: no.

@edithwhoreton: we can't all be Susan Sontag

@edithwhoreton: or even have her as our drug dealer

@lacroixifixion: remember when a*den wrote that un hinged poem about cocaine

@edithwhoreton: cocaine lil and morphine sue forever Susan would be proud

At 7:49PM she turned off her phone. Looked out the window. More of the same. No Natalia. The greenery should have been greener. It all looked dry and dead or dying except for the vines and the apricot trees. Amber turned on her phone again and opened Instagram.

A travel blogger style pic of a kid from high school in Milan.

Sloppy 21st bday pic.

Pretty coffee.

Katie Holmes???

Warren and Bernie meme.

Hot rigatoni pic with Parm and onions.

Mirror selfie.

A cute cat.

A picture of a book to prove literacy.

Some birds.

Peace signs.

Rat in the subway.

Bananas?

Friend sitting in other friend's lap?

Maybe gay.

A menu.

Semi-candid picture in a hallway.

Copies of a litmag.

Mirror pic in a bar.

A homemade omelette with lots of chives on top.

Timothee Chalamet on a red carpet.

Flowers.

Girls at teatime.

The MET.

Infatuation post about hot food.

The great wall of china.

A selfie with Euphoria makeup.

Bikini pic.

Breakfast burrito.

Girl in a bikini eating a breakfast burrito.

A picture of the sky.

A picture of the sky and the ocean.

Concrete and Gucci sneakers.

A dog.

An instagram ad for some online fast fashion store.

Amber turned off her phone and looked out the window. Everything was exactly the same. She stormed the kitchen and felt so alone. Amber grabbed the pitcher of wine and poured some straight down her gullet. Some spilled out of her mouth and stained her cheeks and her chin. She kept gulping.

She felt destabilized. Drunkish. She'd barely started drinking but she'd downed it. She felt drunk. drun runk weren't words. Word. Fuck. Where here her he was as a Natalia? Natalia atalia talia alia lia li I. Natalia natali natal nata nat na a. Natalia. Natalia. Natalia.

Where was—

She turned her phone back on and opened Facebook.
>Three "friends" had birthdays.
>Princeton was posting about upcoming orientation.
>Her mom's friend was ranting about 45.
>Bluestocking book book event.
>McNally Jackson book event.
>A fucking Strand book event.
>Food52 posted about a life-changing flourless chocolate cake.
>A dog getting a haircut.

At 8:03PM she shut her phone off and left the kitchen.

Phone on again at 8:04PM. WhatsApp: no messages. She sent to Natalia:

>I'm so sorry
>I don't know if I
>I didn't mean to
>I'm really
>Please forgive me if I
>I just
>I love you so much
>Please nat please respond
>I feel crazy rn I don't know what to do
>I feel like I've invented you and us and
>I just
>Yeah like idk like I just I
>I love you
>So like

>
> Cool beans
>
> I hope
>
> Fuck
>
> I hope we can like
>
> Please come back??????

She opened her emails:

> SELF Magazine
>
> Do you pee a lot? Does your vagina smell like fish?
>
> hotels.com: Save 40%
>
> Kate Spade Surprise!
>
> Today on R29
>
> The Dish from Food & Wine
>
> Allure
>
> Gap
>
> Cook This Now
>
> Wiggle your way out of an—.
>
> Brilliant Earth
>
> Keepers of the Land
>
> Scott's Cheap Flights
>
> Readers Choice Awards
>
> Ten Dishes Every Reader Can—.
>
> This haircut—.
>
> Pat McGrath Labs
>
> Buy You Today!
>
> Groupon: $30 Massages!
>
> West Elm
>
> From You Flowers!

Events at GA

Lord + Taylor

Wayfair

academia.edu

AllPosters.com

ShopStyle

Epicurious

StudentRate

Victoria's Secret

GoogleAlert for Evanna Lynch

GoogleAlert for Hank Green

Goldstar

Good housekeeping

The New Yorker

Teen Vogue

Condé Nast Traveler

Bookperk

Gilt

Spacelend Presents

Vintage Luxe

These tables make great—.

Spend your Saturday—

New arrivals!

Epicurious

She x-ed out of her emails and opened her camera roll. Her body felt warm when she scrolled passed pics of her with Emma and anyone kind.

But she hadn't come for happy memories; she searched for the bad.

She found photos of her with Charlie—she wanted to punch the past version of herself, smack in the face.

Images of her dancing at frat parties with Laney and Robby. The first dinner they all had together. Robby half-asleep in her dorm. Them all drinking wine from mugs, and eating Cheetos and drinking Smirnoff Ice and smoking cigarettes and weed. And doing shrooms in a New Jersey field, thinking about how living is just ignoring the trash we've made and will soon become.

Amber thought of the trash she was creating. The electrical waste she generated every time she charged her damn phone and scrolled through Twitter. Her vomit would go straight in the Tyrrhenian Sea. Lil fishies and guppies fed by her disease.

One of the first times they got drunk together, when they exchanged their traumatic tales for closeness, Charlie had told her that his mind made him think of New Jersey landfills every time he came. He explained how he had some sort of inferiority complex about the state. When he forced her to fuck, he was thinking of rotted trash and discarded plastic—a land filled with human waste while he was wasting her life away way ay a.

Now she wondered if whoever he was fucking always felt like trash rash ash as a. She wished he would get crabs. The little louse could feed on his blood. Translucent, yellowish bodies overtaking his body and protecting the disposed and the wasted fast-forgotten landfilling junk from being used to help him be done with whoever he next used as a human receptacle.

She deleted every photo of Charlie and Laney and Robby.

She didn't feel cleansed or pure. She felt ugly and empty and wanted to eat his blood like a little crab. To bite down on his skin and make him bleed. She couldn't imagine that any animal would want to live in Charlie, even if they liked living in bush or lash. She wanted to be a crab and prick open his skinholes, claiming his blood. Maybe then he'd let go of her mind.

He was in Memphis. Likely eating barbecue every night. Chicken and nachos, beers and bad wine. And Laney and Robby still defended him. They were in New York posting Instagram pics of—Amber had to check their Instagram. She had blocked them on her finsta, but only soft-blocked them on her rinsta. She craved that access.

Côtes de Boeuf at Augustine. Gin and tonics. Bad music at Berlin. Catch. Per Se. Glitter makeup and vodka shots at Mood Ring. Eleven Madison Park. Le Coucou. Driving Miss Crazy night at the Boiler Room. Five Guys post-McKittrick Hotel. Club Cumming for comedy with Cat Cohen. Club Cumming Cumming. Were they coming to Club Cumming? Where was Alan Cumming was he coming? He wasn't cumming yet. She wasn't cumming. Would she ever cum again? Could she ever? Um she he she could would never ever never come cum she hadn't won that one she had lost had ha she he had ad lost her body bod he had ha he had made her mad he had made her mad he had made her lose her body bod her body bod od. She was so hung rye hungry.

She WhatsApp called Natalia. No answer. She wanted to scream. To cry. She was so ANGRY. SO FUCKING ANGRY. HOW THE FUCK WAS NATALIA SUPPOSED TO EXPECT AMBER TO JUST—WHAT THE FUCK. SHE JUST LEFT HER THERE—ABANDONED HER. THAT'S FUCKING FUCKED UP. THEY WERE BOTH LEFT IN CHARGE OF THE HOUSE—AT LEAST FOR FUCKING LIKE MARCO AND ALESSANDRA AND FUCKING THAT FUCKING FUCKER LUCA FUCKER like what the fucking heck they had said I love you? I love you yo o oh she he had ha — she he had ad thought though they hey had ha meant mean I love you yo o oh what hat ha a fucking twat wat at a.

She was back in her room. Ate her dark ark chocolate nuts & sea salt Kind bar in four bites. It was sticky and soft enough, but crunchy and perfect. The almond & coconut bar went next. She cracked each cashew from the snack pack open with her teeth before chomping them into a mushy mess. She could make cashew milk. Her eyes were so big. A whole hole ole bar of dark chocolate. She ate it square by square.

It tasted kind of nice coming back up. Like she got to eat the chocolate all over again. But she wished she'd had bread or something so she wasn't just spitting up what became, essentially, chunky chocolate syrup. Coarse and slimy. Nuts scratched her esophagus. Disgusting.

She washed her hands, and splashed water on her face to clean off any food remnants before they got too comfortable. She looked herself in the mirror and saw her face. Her eyes were red and glassy. Her nose was crusted over with blood and snot. Her shadow mustache was growing back ack—she checked her chest. Her body was chasing her. She ran her fingers through her hair, and realized she was nothing now, but a human comb.

Home. She he had ha to get et home.

She found her computer left out on her bed. Norwegian Air flights lights light to New ew York. When hen he could she leave? She clicked the week's cheapest flight and her computer remembered her credit card and she clicked some images she didn't look at really and the computer must've realized she was crazed enough not to be a bot on the fritz ritz it's a shame sham ham am oh she's he's so hungry.

Time-stamped at 8:33PM, she WhatsApp'd Natalia:

Please lease ease cum back ack

Let's just jus us u cuddle

don't make me cry

I booked a flight light aight I c u don't care

I love you so much

I thought you would cure me

I'm sorry

Then opened her Messages and texted her parents:

Im coming home soon

All okay

Sorry for weird text

Will be back soon

Coco

She went to the kitchen on a mission. She'd been itching for some non-figgy jam.

She took it from the fridge ridge and popped off its cap and tore off a hunk hun un of bread read that'd that hat at a been bee left on the he table able. She dug her fingers in and fingered out minty mint min in blackberryish goodness foodness and funneled it straight into her mouthhole. She moaned and shoveled bread in right after. Her mouth was so full she could have choked and should have spit pit pi it all out.

Natalia didn't love her. She he thought though hough she loved her. There here her e was no one now ow. She's he's he so o sick sic now ow o. She's he was as burning urning up. She he burns urn her he up. Burn urn her er up. Burn her. Urn he. Yearn year yea ye for her er.

Wine win in the fridge ridge. She drank rank ran an some more straight from fro the he pitcher. Chug! Chug! Chug! Hug! Hug! Hug! Ugh! Ugh! She wanted to throw up—

No. She wouldn't let herself. Not this time. She wasn't going to starve to fucking death in fucking Italy godfuckingdammit what the fucking living hell is this? Fuck that. And fuck Natalia. Why had Natalia left her here all alone? Fuck Natalia. She wanted to fuck Natalia. Fuck, Natalia. Had she made her all up? She was fucking crazy, she looked craz y razy lazy she needed calories.

A bag of Taralli. She chomped them down. A package of biscotti. The chunks of almond and the crumbly goodness. More wine to help it go down. She finished off the pitcher. A beer! Wheat heat eat the beer bee drink rink ink the beer she was delirious. She finished the beer. She opened another. She drank some more and felt calmer.

It was only 8:58PM and all this had happened. She had lost all she'd found she was fond of. She cracked racked open pen en another cold old one and opened her messages. She typed again to Charlie:

> I could tell the people at Fulbright what you did

This time she pressed send.

Her stomach was queasy; there's too to o much inside. Stuffed like a pig pi, full of herself. Herself is inside and an a she he can't get her he e out, she he e wants want wan an a to get out. She's rabid, she's rage rag ra a. She's anxious and an a scared scare care car ca. She he e wants want ant an a to come com co o up and an a get et e out? She's gagging. Her er reflux is reflex, that's not no o a flex lex ex e says ays ay a ex she's he's he just jus us u saying the truth ruth.

She can't go back. Now no p ow she he wanted want ed wan an to go back ack.

She he went ent to enter her er room. She he went ent to her er bed ed. She he was as so tired tire and she felt so queasy easy now. She he curled up. She he didn't wanna hurl url up. She he stayed there here her he curled up like a cat at @ and an she he pulled out her he phone hone one on and an she he opened her er feed fee fe and then hen fell ell el asleep sleep she he wouldn't remember ember but bu eyes eye ey y wide open pen en e she he e met et e god go o and an a knew new ew e both bot good goo go o and an a evil vil vi and an a she he felt

Part II

I just finished eating Peter and washed him down with beer—lager beer. He was tender and juicy—succulent—sugar cured and lean.

I swallowed his heart whole. Sucked his bones clean—leaving them in a pile— neatly stacked—marrowless.

Of his hair I'll weave a silken jerkin—a scarf— to wrap around my throat and a sash.

Of his bones I'll build a bed—spend hours lying upon it—dreaming—his skull a pillow for my head—the birds will come there and find me dead.

They will peck me tearing tiny morsels of flesh. Some will fly away—dropping me into the sea—for fish. The sun will dry me out and the wind scatter flakes of dust over the earth.

Slowly our bones will pulverize as we gradually become powdery—the rain blending us together—washed across the earth in tiny rivulets—seeping down to the roots of the trees—grass—flowers.

They will find our skulls—the last to go—clasped jaw to jaw—in caricature of a kiss.

—Herbert Huncke

When Natalia saw Amber had left the grass, she had been relieved. Amber made it off the ground. Thank God, she'd been wrong; Amber hadn't been so dehydrated she couldn't wake up. She was okay, and everything was going to be fine, and Natalia would never have to come back to the Podere after this summer. Amber made her forget there would be a time beyond the present—made her want to drink in the moments, like they couldn't be retained.

But then Natalia remembered that she hadn't left a note explaining why she had left—that she went to fetch help. Natalia was so swept up with worry when she left, she hadn't been thinking straight. She wondered if Amber would be mad at her. It had only been out of worry—.

Inside the Podere, Natalia called out, "Amber??" But was met with silence. She quietly placed foot after foot, and started running once she saw the mess in kitchen.

"AMBER!" Natalia screamed, "AMBER?!?!!?! COME DOWN! I GOT A CAR!"

Sweat fell down her neck. Her brain sped.

Foot after foot. Breath after breath. Room after room, heading for Amber's.

No Amber. No Amber.

She knocked on her door.

"Amber—. It's me—. A car's coming. Are you hearing me?? They can help—. This isn't funny—I'm—I'm coming in," Natalia said as she pushed open the door—

Only to find Amber, lifeless, covered in vomit. She refused to believe her eyes. She collapsed onto her, clinging onto her dear Amber, begging her to wake, praying for her life. Her ears rung. She tried to shake her to life, but eventually, she resigned to cradling Amber's body. The small spoon she'd never get to cuddle like this again. The wide world lost sound and color. It could have been days or seconds that passed. She nestled herself into Amber, felt the vomit get caught in her hair.

She should call the police. She should charge her phone. Should she call the police? She didn't want to let her go. To make it real. To let them take her away.

Her phone powered back to life.

    WhatsApp Alert: message from Amber

    WhatsApp Alert: message from Amber

    WhatsApp Alert: message from Amber

    WhatsApp Alert: message from Amber

    WhatsApp Alert: message from Amber

    WhatsApp Alert: message from Amber

    WhatsApp Alert: message from Amber

    WhatsApp Alert: message from Amber

    WhatsApp Alert: message from Amber

    WhatsApp Alert: message from Amber

    WhatsApp Alert: message from Amber

    WhatsApp Alert: message from Amber

    WhatsApp Alert: message from Amber

    WhatsApp Alert: message from Amber

    WhatsApp Alert: message from Amber

    WhatsApp Alert: message from Amber

    WhatsApp Alert: message from Amber

    WhatsApp Alert: message from Amber

    WhatsApp Alert: message from Amber

    WhatsApp Alert: message from Amber

    WhatsApp Alert: message from Amber

    WhatsApp Alert: message from Amber

WhatsApp Alert: message from Amber

WhatsApp Alert: message from Amber

WhatsApp Alert: message from Amber

WhatsApp Alert: message from Amber

WhatsApp Alert: message from Amber

WhatsApp Alert: message from Amber

WhatsApp Alert: message from Amber

WhatsApp Alert: message from Amber

WhatsApp Alert: message from Amber

Natalia shook like her body had broken, or was malfunctioning. An earthquake within herself. Amber had been so out of it when she had gone to fetch help. When Amber had awoken, she likely felt abandoned and alone. Natalia had left her on her own. How could she? She should have done something. Left a note. Something. Anything. Amber had been so dehydrated and malnourished. Her brain wasn't functioning normally.

Amber died delirious, and probably hating her.

Natalia's heart was cracking. Harder. Wider.

She cried into her phone and cradled it close to her heart and let the coolness of its metal calm her.

> I'm so sorry

What??

> I don't know if I
>
> I didn't mean to
>
> I'm really
>
> Please forgive me if I

Amber died thinking she was mad at her.

> I just

> I love you so much

She loved her. She loved her. But she loved her, too.

Natalia wanted to smash her phone on the floor.

> Please nat please respond
>
> I feel crazy rn I don't know what to do
>
> I feel like I've invented you and us and
>
> I just
>
> Yeah like idk like I just I

She should have just stayed and charged her phone and called an ambulance. She had been so scared Amber was dying, she felt like she had to leave and find help. She hadn't been thinking straight. She fled, and that's what killed her. Natalia killed her.

> I love you

She killed her sweet Amber.

> So like

There was a honk outside. Fuck, the car.

> Cool beans
>
> I hope
>
> Fuck
>
> I hope we can like

The police would question her.

> Please come back??????
>
> Please lease ease cum back ack
>
> Let's just jus us u cuddle

Amber was—

> don't make me cry

> I booked a flight light aight I c u don't care

Amber thought Natalia wanted her gone.

> I love you so much

"I love you," Natalia said.

> I thought you would cure me

Her mind stopped yelling. They were back in the kitchen kissing and consuming.

Amber had wanted Natalia to cure her.

> I'm sorry

"Natalia?" a man called from outside. He knocked on the door. She froze in place, and didn't answer. "Sto entrando!" She could hear the front door click open.

Hands on face, feeling for fluids. Sweat filled her hair. She smacked hands on cheeks as she called out "Ciao, ciao," and slammed the door behind her. She refused to let him find out.

She greeted the neighbor downstairs, and stopped his forward motion with a grateful-seeming hug. She worried she smelled of death, and so explained that Amber had food poisoning, and that was that. She'd be fine.

He expressed his concern while Natalia hid her hands behind her back so he wouldn't see them shake.

He insisted he could stay until Amber felt better. He explained that he had children, he knew how to deal with these things. He began up the steps, when Natalia grabbed him by his shoulders and pulled him into an embrace.

"Grazie," she said, and he held her as she cried. His arms around her felt so comfortable. She felt so protected and safe and she didn't want him to leave, but she knew she needed him to go. She told him she had been so worried that Amber was not okay, but she was okay, and she was just so relieved. She insisted that's why she was crying. And she was crying so hard he believed her.

He assured her everything was fine now, and she was a good friend for getting help and caring so much, and Natalia listened to him.

Natalia rubbed her face dry and pulled away from him. She asked him to leave, saying she needed to rest. It had been such a stressful night. He asked again if he shouldn't go check on Amber, but Natalia said that would only embarrass her.

He agreed to leave when Natalia promised to call if the situation worsened. She locked the door behind him when he left, and she laughed, in shock. She was safe. He was gone.

She walked the same route from the entrance to Amber's room as she did before. She felt sick remembering how she yelled at Amber, begging her to come down and get in the car. She'd been Schrodinger's Cat. Dead and alive, both at once. All possibilities were truths. Amber could have been asleep. In her own pile of beer and bile and spit.

When she reached the bed, she searched for any sign of animation in Amber's eyes.

"Are you here?" she asked.

Of course, Amber couldn't answer. But outside, the wind picked up a bit. Not as it would have in some stupid film, just a normal amount, especially considering the sky before, the day's weather. Natalia had worried there would be hail. Thinking of storms while looking at Amber's face, red and bloated, crusted over with drying vomit—. To be alive is to be stupid.

She picked off the flakes of puke, and wiped Amber clean with the remainder of her makeup remover wipes. The smell was sickly and sweet, and bits of Amber's vomit got stuck and forgotten on the back of Natalia's elbow.

Natalia sat back on the bed beside Amber and tried to memorize her every feature. Her eyes were glassy like a doll's. Or a dead girl's. She had shadow smile lines along with a whisper of a wrinkle on her forehead. Her eyebrows were overgrown. Natalia wanted to count every hair on her body.

Amber was quickly losing heat.

Natalia slowed her breath as much as she could, trying to keep her chest from moving, so it'd stay still and aligned with Amber's breathless body. She traced her finger over Amber's face, and down her body. If she didn't call the police now, she'd never be able to. They'd assume it was some tawdry exchange-student murder situation surely. But if she called them, it would become real. Amber would be taken from her and sent back home to her family. It would be like they had never happened, and Amber would be gone.

She bit her lip and remembered her promise.

Her heart felt hollow and empty; alone. She craved to have Amber's fingers inside her just once more. She clung to the body, as if their physical closeness might somehow revive her.

She felt like a kid up past their bedtime; unsupervised. She looked at Amber and asked, "What do you want me to do?" Before she fell asleep with her head rested on Amber's chest.

In her sleep, Natalia spoke to Amber directly, who told her exactly what to do. In the dream, Natalia had agreed, and Amber seemed relieved. But in the morning sun, the dream made Natalia feel she'd made some deal with the devil.

She couldn't have been asleep for more than an hour or two. But she stayed in bed for a while and tried to imagine how she could even do it, practically speaking. She didn't want to do it. She only felt obligated because she knew Amber, and she knew in every cell of her body this is what she wanted. She would have to stop thinking of her as Amber, though. It would be too much to understand what she was doing as she did it. She would focus on the small steps, logistics, and ignore the big picture. If she thought of the big picture, she wouldn't be able to complete the puzzle. Though it wasn't a puzzle she was piecing together, more like one she'd be taking apart. But the whole idea of their two bodies joined was predicated on the belief that it was a marrying of spirits that manifested in this physical re-union. A marriage, not morte. A Fontanian cut through to the next dimension.

That was it.

She straddled Amber's body, and hugged her, holding her, getting a solid grip around her torso, clutching her neck. She carried her like a man with his wife on their wedding day. To the bathroom.

She laid her down in the tub. She searched for something sharp. Nail clippers wouldn't do, but the miniature scissors just might. She grabbed her phone and Google searched for major arteries. Lots of images popped up. She stabbed Amber like a rogue acupuncturist, cleansing Amber of her own deoxygenated blood. Her skin was thicker than she'd thought. The scissors were sharp, but it took a lot to draw blood.

In time, Natalia became an action painter, made bloody by the memory of Amber. An afterimage of her innards. The bathtub turned red, and Amber became paler, looking more deceased by the moment. Natalia sat and watched her love lose what moved her heart. She didn't even want to cry. She felt like she was watching a movie—watching herself. She turned on the faucet, let the water cleanse the tub, cleanse her body. Natalia wet her hands, and ran them over Amber's forehead, moving the hair from Amber's face. It took longer than she thought it would for the blood to drain. There was so much.

Getting a solid hold on Amber's now-slick body was the hardest part. It had been easier to get a grasp from the bed. She had to step into the bath and crouch down to her level to raise her from this cleansing open-coffin. She envied the tub's abiotic innocence. Saltwater drained from Natalia's eyes—a baptistic cleansing.

Natalia's lower back cramped. She held Amber's neck, trying to protect her head from strain. Amber's toes tickled Natalia's thighs as they moved along with her steps. She was straining and sweating, crumbling beneath the dead weight.

She could hear the dogs whining. She forgot to feed them. She realized her stomach was grumbling, too, which only made her feel sicker.

They reached the kitchen, where Natalia clumsily set Amber's body down onto the island, next to the sink. She laid her on the counter so her legs wouldn't dangle. If only Natalia had done more strength training, perhaps she'd have been more prepared. Felt less out of shape.

She went to the sink to pour herself some water. Lifesmells were leaving the room and the deathsmells made her nauseous. She looked out the window and saw how empty the world looked. She couldn't even see the birds. She only heard them, and they sounded frivolous. She shut the blinds and remembered her phone.

She put out the dog food and replenished their water supply. The dogs stormed the room, somehow instinctively knowing they'd been summoned, but they ignored their food. They wouldn't stop barking at Amber.

"Shhhh," Natalia begged, "Basta! Basta!!!" She said, desperate for them to stop.

Carrying their bowls of kibble and water, she physically urged the dogs to follow her outside.

"Bene, bene. Grazie," she said to the dogs as they dove into their meal, forgetting the drama in the kitchen.

Natalia went back inside and locked the door behind her.

Grounds filled the pot. She waited for the coffee to brew.

She tied her hair back into a tight bun and sifted through the family's collection of knives: bread knife, carving knife, chef knife, boning knife, utility knife, filleting knife, steak knife, paring knife.

She selected her mug, and poured herself a nice, fat cup of hot coffee. She drank it black because she wanted to hate herself a little bit. She took massive sips despite its heat. She scalded her mouth, enjoyed the way it burned her.

She allowed herself a look at Amber, who had no color left. Just some punctuated flesh, and skin, stained pink.

"I wish you were here," she said to Amber's face before she downed a second cup like it was a glass filled with straight vodka. It made her the good kind of queasy.

Caffeine high, she returned to the knives, and selected the boning knife. Curvy and flexible. Practically a sex toy.

She needed to knife her. Cut her open.

She wondered if her grandpa found butchering hot. This all felt ordained. This may not have been written in the stars, but in her own DNA. A butcher by blood, she thought, as she took the boning knife to Amber's shoulders and severed her arms from their joints; she split the arms at their elbows. Amber's legs from her pelvis; thighs from calves by her knees. Each broken ligament tougher than the last. It took all her might, but she had to keep going—not stopping to think, or remember the smell—and the blood crystallizing on her hands, all over her body. She kept thinking Amber was going to wake up and yell at her, but she never did.

Natalia kept running the knife under hot water so the lines remained clean and so the blood wouldn't thicken and congeal on the metal. Amber was skinny, obviously, but she hadn't realized how thicc she was, too. Though some of that bloat was undoubtedly due to her death, and the nature of it.

Natalia's heart raced, and she bit her lip so hard it bled; she pleaded with her eyes not to shed more tears. Deep breaths. Coffee and stomach acids danced together in her body.

Amber looked so at peace until Natalia cracked, pulled, cut, forced her head from her neck. That was the worst of it. Natalia couldn't look her in the eyes. She cradled Amber's head like she was her newborn baby, willing Amber back to life.

"Okay, okay," she said to herself.

She placed down the boning knife and washed her hands—blood and innardbits caught in the drain. She noticed blood dripping from her finger, and washed it clean, but soon realized it was her own blood, and not Amber's flowing down the drain now. She stuck her finger in her mouth and sucked the blood out, tasting metallic while she fetched paper towels to stop the bleeding, then covered every surface she could.

Natalia was being watched.

Amber's head, divorced from her body, stared her straight in the eyes.

Natalia's phone rang and she jumped, terrified.

She let it ring once, twice, checked to see who was calling.

Her father.

She had to pick up. He'd be worried if not.

"Hey, Papa," she said.

"No ciao?"

"Oh yeah, sorry. We've all started speaking English because Amber—." Amber. Amber. Amber. Amber—

"Amber?"

"Yeah, she's—here to help with the irrigation," Natalia said. with her eyes glued to Amber's.

"Marco said they've left you there alone to watch over the house and the dogs."

"Yeah, it's just Amber and me," she said.

"It's a shame for them. She's not well, his mother."

"Yeah," Natalia said as she stepped toward Amber's head. She used her free hand to lower her eyelids. Her skin was so fragile and cold. Uncooked chicken skin.

"But you're well? Still having fun? Your mother and I, we are missing you," he said.

"Well, I miss you, too. How's home?" She asked, wanting desperately for him not to answer.

"We're fine. I was just calling to see. Will you be back in time for your mother's birthday? I'm making reservations at Mrs Robinson's," he said.

"Oh, yes. She keeps talking to me about how much I would love the popcorn dessert."

"Their sweetbreads, as well— we liked the place very much. Your brother found it."

"Ah yes, yes." She was talking to her father with blood on her hands.

"So will you be back by then, do you think?" He asked.

"Hm yeah, I'll be back. I'm thinking of returning soon," she said. She hadn't realized till she said it, but she'd have to leave Italy as soon as she was through. She couldn't stay at the Podere any longer than necessary.

"Oh, yes?"

"I like the work, I do, I just—." She had forgotten about the work. The vines and the grapes and the weeds and the dirt and the spiders.

"I'll go ahead and include you in the reservation then."

"Thanks, Papa." Could she ever again look her father in the face?

"Okay, well I will leave you to it, then. I just wanted to make sure before I made the reservation."

"Sounds good. Love you." The last time she'd said I love you was to Amber.

"Liebe dich, Schatz," her father said back, just before he ended the call.

Natalia allowed herself a deep breath, but Amber's deadsmell haunted her nose. Without noticing, she released a shallow "Fuck" with every exhale.

176

She leaned on the countertop and tried to figure out what she was doing. Fuck. Her fingers tapped the granite. She wasn't going to let herself think about the last words Amber had said. Stay focused. Keep to logistics. Be like her grandfather. Be the butcher.

She unlocked her phone and opened Safari, where she searched "recipes," which turned up lots of postings that featured heirloom tomatoes and olives. She refined her search, typing instead, "how to cook a whole—." her fingers lingered, toying with options. The suggestions were chicken, beef tenderloin, fish, chicken in a crock pot, duck, filet mignon, lobster, chicken in an air fryer, chicken in the instant pot, ham. How to cook a whole human.

All right. She would finish butchering and then figure out the rest.

She searched, "human anatomy organs" and took a screenshot.

She'd have to take the organs out first. Natalia vaguely recalled some scientific reason why organ removal helped keep meat from spoiling.

She opened the freezer and searched for room. She wondered if she could safely keep a bicep inside. She moved some ice around, and managed to keep both biceps in the ice bin. She tried to cover the limbs in paper towels, but they clung to the blood, so she opted for plastic wrapping instead, in hopes that the blood wouldn't mark the freezer. She severed Amber's hands from her forearms, and placed her forearms beside the unopened pint of pistachio Talenti.

Amber's feet stood on the granite countertop, detached from their burden: the body. Natalia had never noticed the height of Amber's arches. Her toes, painted purple. Natalia picked up the left foot and felt its calloused heel. Thick and hard, sandpaper-ish.

She placed the bottom of Amber's foot along the side of her head, like an old telephone.

"Brrrring brrrring, brrrirrrng brrrrring. Leave a message after the—beeeeeeeeep. Hey, it's Nat. You there?" She moved the foot inches away from her face, and examined it head-on. She had never been big into foot play, but it was just so funny looking in isolation.

She felt she was living-out a Magritte. Surrealist praxis.

She placed Amber's big left toe in her mouth. Salty, dirty, dehydrated. Fleshlollipop. She placed it back beside its pair. She grabbed Amber's hands—interlacing her fingers between Ambers. She clasped down, wanting to feel her life respond. They twitched as blood spilled out. Her own fingers trembled.

Amber had asked that she be cured. She had to preserve her belly. She had to eat her out of this world. Her last coming. This much she knew.

She turned Amber's torso on its belly, and used the boning knife to slice down her spine—knife bent, pulled out vertebra by vertebra. The knife glided so smoothly, and the blood barely splattered. It felt ordained. Like Amber was holding her hand and her grandfather was guiding her through the process.

She went first for her lungs. Why were organs and innards always so pink and warm? And only blue when deoxygenated? The sky was full of oxygen and blue all the time. Then again, veins, too, looked blue, and oxygen courses through them constantly when functional.

Amber's veins were now blue and starved.

Natalia didn't want to touch Amber's insides. They were slick with fluids. Her hands were stiff and shaking. She could never be a doctor. Maybe a mortician.

Okay. "Okay," she said as she pulled herself together and put down her tool: the knife. She went in with her hands, and held her breath as she clutched Amber's left lung, and tried her best to dislocate it from tissue connecting it to the rest of her body. Wet sounds and acid air.

Once the lung was out of the body, Natalia didn't know what to do with it, so she placed it in the sink. She worried her fingers would break the flesh lining her ribs, though she wasn't sure what harm that would do, really.

She went back for the second lung.

It got easier. Became methodical. She almost forgot how the gaseous smells affected her. Her mind dulled and she became a thoughtless machine, pulling apart a person bit-by-bit.

Natalia kept having to wash her hands and refer back to the image; she found it hard to figure which organ was what. It was shocking to think she held all this inside her, too. That these bits are what kept her alive. And couldn't keep Amber.

She separated Amber's heart, kidneys, livers, bladder, intestines, pancreas, and appendix from her carcass, and placed them in the sink.

The coffee in her stomach whined; it craved companionship. And anyway, the cooking part came next.

She searched the cupboards for soy sauce and fish sauce. Honey, nutmeg, and pepper. Fresh ginger, which she'd sliver. Whiskey. They had no limes.

She whisked it all together in a small, glass bowl.

Parchment paper on a sheet pan.

No, first, plastic baggies. Was that damning? Who cared? She needed them for the marinade.

She took the chef's knife to Amber's rib cage, and painted them with marinade. She placed them in the plastic baggies, and fairly distributed the leftover mix of sauce and season. She sealed the bags shut, and massaged the ribs.

Next up: she didn't know. Nothing looked appetizing. She didn't want to be a cannibal.

Dismembering the body of her loved one made her feel like a man. It made her hate men, and the man she was becoming. She didn't want to be her grandfather.

Amber's belly.

What she set out to do in the first place: cure her.

Salt. Lots of table salt.

She Googled "how to make sodium nitrite." Everything read like real science. She Googled "how to cure without sodium nitrite." The answer was celery powder. She searched "how to make celery powder," which led to her search "how to dehydrate without a dehydrator," which led her to pre-heat the oven to 80 degrees Celsius.

But her belly was hungry, and she couldn't wait for Amber's to cure.

She chopped onions and cried. And not because of the syn-propanethial-S-oxide in the air, though the excuse of onions allowed for distraction that kept Natalia from over-analyzing her current reality.

Oil sizzled. The onions sautéed till translucent. Intestines were sliced into links then boiled, before she crisped them in the pan with the onions. Her shoulders relaxed. It smelled good? Like chicken sausage. Locally-sourced. She covered the pan with its top to allow the meat to cook through without drying out.

Natalia turned the stovetop off and chopped up chives. Sprinkled them on top, along with kosher salt, pepper, and sesame seeds.

If there were shit still stuck inside Amber's entrails, Natalia couldn't taste it. Piping hot and steamy, juicy and well-seasoned. She'd never had a better sausage-substitute in her life. She was thinking of Amber as turkey or duck, a chicken replacement.

Her mind was functioning frenetically. She went from thinking of meats and meals to the new reality of her future. This would be her only surgery. She would never go to med school. She could never reenter society. She would have to leave the Podere once she had finished with Amber. She would have to leave Italy.

The oven beeped. Natalia temporarily abandoned her meal. She grabbed the celery from the fridge, and cleared the aluminum foil from the sheet pan she'd taken out. She separated the stalks and placed the pan in the oven.

In the meantime, back to her meal. When she thought of it as eating Amber, it made her want to throw up, which felt ironic and bad. If Amber had cannibalized her, she wouldn't want her to gag her way through it. She should relish every bite. To accomplish this, she tried to shoo Amber from her mind, which also felt wrong.

Lucky for Natalia, only half a plate in she couldn't stop thinking as Amber. Not of Amber, but as her. With each munch and chew, she recalled throwing up: comfy cats @s and pink.

She was gagging. Not on Amber…but as Amber. She couldn't process it intellectually, but she felt it in her bones. It wasn't scary, or even overwhelming. It felt full and beautiful. Like she was complete.

Natalia had to throw up. She glued her lips shut—she couldn't let Amber go like this. They were so close to true togetherness.

She looked at the pan. She dropped the fork and shoveled the rest into her mouth with her hands. She turned the stovetop back on and cooked the rest of the intestines the same way. Her face was covered with schmutz when she finished. She ran the sink and placed her face in way of the water, cleaning herself off inches from Amber's uncooked organs.

She felt drunk on the thoughts of Amber. Her brain felt schizophrenic. She wanted to check her phone, but not her own phone. Amber's phone.

She should text Emma as Amber. See if she's okay. And her mother.

No, she should keep cooking.

She should text Alessandra and see how they're doing. When they were coming back.

Natalia had to figure out what the hell she was going to do—.

She needed to cook all of Amber as soon as possible.

She'd have to clean and leave no trace by the time they return. Luca never even mentioned his grandmother. They couldn't have been that close. She could make him come back and care for the place.

Air escaped the fatty entrails as they came to a crisp.

She turned off the stovetop, and went to the fridge to fetch a beer. She cracked off its cap, and downed half the bottle. She needed alcohol for this. She was thirsty, and her mind craved numbness.

The pan cooled just enough so she could shovel down the intestines. She wasn't hungry but her body wanted to finish consuming Amber. She wouldn't stop eating until she was done.

Amber tasted like oysters: briny, but sweet.

She'd like to prepare a peach galette and substitute Amber for the peaches, but the thought of flesh and crumble did not please the mind of her gullet.

"How to make bone broth" Natalia Googled. She searched the pantry for apple cider vinegar, which she found.

She took Amber's limbs from the freezer, and picked back up the boning knife. The flesh had become tense, which made cutting into it, searching for bones less messy.

Into the now boiling water went Amber's femur, fibula, tibia, patella, and humerus, cervical, thoracic, and lumbar vertebrae, sacrum, coccyx, clavicle, scapula, carpals, metacarpals, hip bones, phalanges, tarsals, metatarsals, and sternum. She forced them to fit.

Her stomach grumbled, unhappy. It was overwhelming how much Amber there was, scattered about the kitchen. Bits of her everywhere. Natalia felt surrounded and small. Blood rushed to her cheeks.

Her own body was grimy—her skin felt like a suit that belonged to someone, but not herself. The cooking was taking a toll on her body, not just Amber's. Everything cooking still needed more time.

She cleaned the tub, bleaching it white.

She needed to pack. She put on clothes and shoved everything else into her suitcase or into the trash. Her computer. Clothes. Underwear. Tampons. Who cared?

She knew she'd told her father she'd be home soon, but things were changing now, and everything felt more inevitable and impossible at once. She wasn't herself as they had known her, she was becoming one with Amber—no, she wouldn't be able to celebrate her mother's birthday, or even look her straight in the eyes.

She went to Amber's room and grabbed her phone. Password protected. Shit. And then she remembered. Facial recognition. Down to the kitchen. Would Apple store the image of Amber's head, severed?

Natalia opened the texts from Amber's mother first:

> Amber, honey, are you all right? Is everything ok?
>
> Your texts are worrying me and not making much sense
>
> Your father and I have tried calling you and you aren't picking up.
>
> We love you so much and are happy to have you home soon.

Natalia texted as Amber:

> Hey ! Sorry to scare you !!
>
> All good all good
>
> Food poisoning
>
> I did book a flight
>
> but they're letting me move it
>
> And not charging extra
>
> so gonna stay longer, I think
>
> Sorry for the confusion
>
> I love you sm

> Are you around for a call?

We miss your voice

                                                Ah I wish I'm so sorry

                          I'm supposed to be working right now

Maybe later

                                                        Yeah definitely

I'll try you tonight

              They are being a little weird about how much wifi I'm using

                                     Maybe we can wait a few days?

                                                            I'm so sorry

                                               I love and miss you

Okay —

If they're not treating you well,

your father and I will pay for a hotel somewhere

                                                           No no all good

                                                           Thanks mom

                                                               Love you

                                                         Really have to go

Ok! Xoxo

                                                                     Xoxo

Miss my coco

                                                         Miss you too

Oh I miss you! But I meant how you always mistype it

                                                     Oh yes, of course.

                                      I switched it in autocorrect

                                                                Xoxo

Nice! Well, anyway, coco and xoxo!

Don't forget sunscreen!

Natalia wiped her face dry, as she opened Amber's texts from Emma:

> Dude she moved all her stuff out
>
> Im sobbing I hate this
>
> Also confession
>
> We had break-up sex
>
> I topped
>
> It was pretty hot ngl

Natalia typed:

> Nooooooo
>
> I mean
>
> Love to hear it
>
> And hate to hear it

She had no clue what to say. She felt guilty for being on Amber's phone, taking over her conversations—that's what she had to do. Speak as her, not for her. The whole point of all of this was so that Amber wouldn't disappear with her death; she would live on through Natalia.

She closed out of Amber's Messages. Went to her e-mails and found the flight confirmation. It left in three days. A red-eye from FCO to JFK.

Though Natalia had never been to New York, she felt its memory throb into her out from her gut. Central Park, the MET, Frick, the Whitney, and Amber's mailman, who had been on their route for as long as she could remember—.

Amber had never told Natalia about her mailman.

His greying hair and kind eyes, the Hello Kitty pillow he gave to Amber one Christmas. Natalia's heartbeat picked up. Her hands moistened.

Amber could still go. They could both go together.

She had an overwhelming vision of Amber standing across the street from Central Park.

The light switched from Walk to Stop back to Walk again. Amber crossed the street and sat on a bench. Maybe she did believe in free will.

"Oh my God," she whispered.

Amber was telling her to go to New York City.

Amber was telling her.

"I love you," she was telling her.

She was her.

She was telling herself.

She was they.

They were telling each other to go to New York City.

They were telling themselves to go to New York City.

If they were going to New York City in three days, Natalia would have to work quickly. She went back to the kitchen, and turned up the oven. She threw the ribs on a sheet pan, next to the celery.

She chopped the deboned leg and arm flesh into inch thick chunks. She coated the meat with flour and pepper, before braising it in a pan lined with olive oil. She watched over each individual piece, turning them on their sides to ensure uniform browning.

Once all of the meat was properly done, she cleared the pot and added vinegar and wine, which she found in the pantry. It was bottled, but from the Podere's personal collection. Seemed to be a slight vintage. She saved some of it for drinking. She found bay leaves by the spices, and threw a few in before adding water. Once boiling, she threw Amber's limbmeat back into the pot before she placed the lid on top.

She rinsed off the knife and returned to the cutting board. There, she cut potatoes, carrots, and onions into stew-appropriate sizes.

She had time to kill before she could add them to the pot. She still didn't know what to do with Amber's other organs, face, hands, and feet. She should have shaved her before starting all this. If only she'd been a bigger fan of Hannibal, perhaps she'd have been more prepared.

She pulled out her phone and searched "Hannibal craziest meals." Business Insider went off on this tongue he cooked in season one. She had totally forgotten about Amber's tongue. She searched tongue recipes, and found an easy one for offal which just required allspice, bay leaves, salt, pepper, beef broth, and butter. She'd let it simmer in a pan for a few hours till tender.

Ten hours hadn't passed, but she took the celery out of the oven. Her memory and Google-checking made it clear it required more time than she had to cure. She would do her best, and eat it nonetheless.

She blended the celery, which was a little moist, but somewhat powdery, then blended it in with the table salt. Sugar and spices. She salted Amber's fatty stomach. It would have been bigger a week prior, pre-near starvation. Wrapped her stomach into a roll, held it together with more twine. Natalia would consume the totality of Amber's unspent calories—that was her mission. To become what she ate: Amber—or one with her.

Stomach in fridge.

On to the organs. Amber's heart glared at her. A purpled burgundy.

She placed the other organs in the fridge to help them keep.

Google said warm puffin heart was a delicacy, but it had to be freshly-hunted. She found, instead, a beef heart recipe that seemed more promising. She cleaned out the arteries and blood vessels, trimmed off some fat. Tied it up with cooking twine three times crosswise, and pan-seared it two minutes each side. To finish, she baked it in the oven for fifteen minutes or so.

She set herself a placemat and poured herself a glass of wine. It was just past one. She was making good progress. She set an intention for this next meal. To relish in the knowledge her body would soon be fueled by Amber's heart.

The heart came out perfectly medium rare. She used a steak knife to cut in. It felt fragile to the touch of her utensils, but perhaps that was her own rigidity projected onto the heart. When it hit her mouth, it practically evaporated. Butter. She'd never tasted anything so rich and tender at once. Carnivoristic ecstasy. She couldn't swallow each bite fast enough—though she tried to pace herself, to properly let each cut of her love melt onto her tongue. She felt the proteins disintegrate and become one with her saliva. Traveled down her throat; the heart found home in her gullet. Her stomach throbbed, but not in ache or pain—with life. Her stomach beat with Amber's heart, reunited in a body alive.

She carried the fallen juices with the last piece of aorta. Her eyes closed as she chewed— but just before she could swallow, her throat tensed up. Her gut tightened. Natalia unconsciously grabbed the side of her torso, half-hugging herself, half-feeling herself up to see how fat or skinny she was. She wondered how her belly fat would compare to Amber's, and she hated herself for wondering that. She wondered how it'd look once she consumed Amber's stomach.

Her skin felt like it had lost collagen. Like she was growing, aging. She was young in this body, even though she wasn't. The world had seen her youth and sucked its sap right out of her, filling her instead with one shitty man. What man?

She had never known a Charlie, and Amber had never mentioned him. But she could feel memory of him in her body now. She felt him in her body, too, gagged by his cock. She remembered what she'd never seen: Charlie undid his belt, unzipped his jeans. Hard underneath his boxers. He pulled them down, and nudged himself closer. Amber was force-fed. He forced down his cum. Wanted her to swallow. She closed her eyes, and imagined she was nowhere. In the land of grainy greyness. Dissolved from the responsibilities of corporeality.

She swallowed.

One of Natalia's timers chirped, bringing her back to the present. She took a sip of wine, to sober up. She pulled the ribs from the oven. She found this access to Amber's own archive of experience dizzying and addictive. The hours felt like minutes.

The ribs smelled of meat, sweet, and acid. She threw as many as would fit comfortably on to her plate, and didn't wait for them to cool.

She tore through them—the pangs of ginger mixed with the umami of the fish sauce with nutmeg led to a sweet caramelized coating. Her lips dripped honey. That crisped and subtly charred layer protected the meat closest to the bone from drying out, trapping any moisture inside. Bone from her bones, flesh from her flesh. From the ribs of Amber, Natalia felt herself sustained. With every bite, she imagined kissing Amber's breasts, chest, ribs, stomach before she would eat her out to completion.

When she finished, she added the onions, carrots, and potatoes into the stew to liven up and play with the richness of the meat juices.

She washed her dirtied dishes, pans, pots, and utensils. The artificial-smelling fake-lemon-scented dish detergent cleared her nostrils. A palate-cleanser.

She noticed slowly rotting apricots on the countertop nearest the fridge. Natalia liked how they were never quite satisfying, just giving a hint of wet, saccharine deliciousness, but Amber oiled her mind.

Natalia recalled Amber's first night at the Podere. She hadn't even remembered grabbing for apricots, but she had access now to herself remembered.

Everyone had left the room, only the two of them remained. Amber and Natalia, alone, surrounded by the relics of the family to which neither of them belonged. Natalia had reached over to the bowl in the center of the table and grabbed three apricots. She placed one between her lips, bit in to separate its flesh from the pit.

By the end of the day, Natalia had eaten the stew, Amber's tongue, and had followed a recipe for lamb kidneys, which used mustard, lemon, shallots, parsley, and white wine. She ate the kidneys, then decided that was enough Amber consumption for one day. Not only did her body feel heavy and overstuffed, but her head felt tired of fighting for authority.

With every bite, she seemed to gain more and more insight into Amber's life. She'd somehow remember some detail, place, person, or moment as though it was her own memory. Some were painless and pointless. She'd remember a paper she wrote on Auden or Oscar Wilde. An episode of *Schitt's Creek* or, unfortunately, *The Goldbergs*. Jesus, she couldn't believe she watched that crap. She remembered a nightmare Amber must have had in which a house was haunting Amber. When she ate her liver, she tasted tiramisu. When she cut her tongue, she saw Fontana. When she saw Fontana, she wanted to cut. When she remembered Charlie, she wanted to cut him wide open and harm him. She could picture his face clearly now, not just his pink little dick. She wanted to crack a raw egg on his head. Break the yolk and stain him. She imagined slicing his throat, but not before choking him on one of her cocks.

Feeling what happened made everything so clear. She should have insisted Amber go to that hospital that doctor mentioned in the show. The one that helped patients with rumination syndrome. As Natalia chewed over Amber's body parts, she could see so clearly how Charlie had turned Amber to nothing. She stopped eating when Amber's memory made her recall sweet vomit tastes in the bathroom of the Borghese.

Natalia put the bone broth in the fridge and gave Amber's bones to the dogs, hoping their spit would help emulsify the evidence, so she wouldn't have to try so hard to hide her bones. They'd surely be found eventually. She just needed to make it to New York before that happened.

She stored Amber's face, brain, liver, lungs, breasts, butt, hands, feet, and pelvis in the fridge or the freezer, wherever she could fit them.

She brushed her teeth twice that night, trying to clear her mouth's memory of Amber's flesh, perhaps so it could better remember the taste of her spit.

She stared at herself in the mirror for a long while. Searching for signs of difference. Notes of Amber. Her image reflected back as it always had. Though she started to see more of Amber's anxiousness on her face. Her hair looked curlier, too. Like the nerves had twisted her follicles. She enjoyed her image mirroring Amber's likeness. She became Amber's creation. And yet Natalia's body so quickly became Amber's whole world. The real world had led Amber to death. And now, out of the simplicity and purity of her devotion to Amber, here was Natalia, following in her footsteps.

That night, she tried to sleep, but nerves kept her awake. She instinctively lay in Amber's bed and stared at the ceiling. She wondered if occupying her space and holding her body inside her own made her more Amber than Natalia. Her mind had been subsumed. She barely remembered what used to occupy her brainholes and time.

She felt bitter to be the body left behind. Every sound she heard was a threat. She was surprised Alessandra hadn't called to check in on things. She had no idea what she would do. She had to let her know she'd be leaving, but that felt so comical and pointless. She tensed to the creaks of the hardwood floor and the rustling of the wind outside instead of sleeping, the groaning pipes and imagined noiseless sirens. She remembered the night prior, when she'd left the door unlocked—she'd remembered to lock the door. She had triple-checked before retreating to the bedroom.

She imagined what would happen if Alessandra had someone check on her tomorrow, and discovered what she'd done. She pictured Amber's severed body magically reanimating piece-by-piece. If she could gain empathy through eating, she wondered if Amber felt her own consumption, even when dead. Could her ghost feel Natalia bite down on her tongue, scraping Amber's tastebuds with her teeth one last time?

When Natalia held Amber's hand in the kitchen—she imagined Amber squeezing back.

Eventually, she fell asleep. She dreamt of New York City. It felt like Amber was guiding her on this path. She felt so warm and full, she couldn't bear it—she had never felt so complete.

When she woke, it was dark still, and her vision grainy. Atmospheric fluctuations made stagnant air feel rushed, and led to window-made crunkling.

Her stomach felt solid and unshakeable. But she wanted this over with. Despite the effectiveness of her work thus far, Natalia did not enjoy eating her lover's flesh. Now, it was more of a compulsion. Her own body would quit basic functions did she not continue.

She went downstairs and checked on the bones. The dogs had done some damage, but she'd let them gnaw away at them for the day in hopes they wouldn't look human when they were through. Then she could bury them somewhere the dogs wouldn't dig them up. At least not till she was long gone, anyway.

Natalia threw down some kibble and water, but this time put down more water and less kibble, so the dogs would focus on Amber's marrow.

In the kitchen, she warmed the bone broth on the stovetop as she prepared herself coffee. She sipped her liquids side-by-side. One gave her energy, the other depleted it as it made her see Charlie as Amber had, for the first time after everything had happened.

Natalia rinsed the liver and the lungs, then sliced them into small, even-sized pieces. Placed them in a bowl to soak in milk. Warmed butter in a skillet. Coated liver in flour, pepper, and salt. Fried till crisped and browned, to-taste. Increased heat to medium and cooked for another ten minutes or so, till the pan whistled for her attention. Topped off with lemon and a pinch of salt.

She ate it hot and saw nothing she hadn't seen all ready. She only saw Charlie, and wanted to cry, to harm him, for haunting Amber even in death.

She couldn't find any recipes that used a bladder, let alone a uterus. She whispered a prayed apology to Amber, as she brought it outside and fed it to the dogs. She needed the evidence of Amber's body disappeared fast.

She warmed milk and added it to her now-cold coffee. Natalia never drank milk in anything, and liked the grit of the grounds in her coffee, generally. Her tastes were not her own anymore. Her brain went warm and fuzzy, her vision purple and pink. The connection was complete now. She almost blacked out on the feeling of warmth and closeness.

She doused A1 sauce on Amber's breasts, butt, hands, feet, and pelvis and thought of her alive. Her concern and softness. She missed being with her, even as she became her.

The sheet pan went into the oven, set to high heat.

Natalia went outside bearing Amber's head, a proper Caravaggian Goliath, in search of garden tools—a hammer or something—to help her gain access to Amber's brain. Blood, guts, brain damage galore. Smash, bang, clunk.

She first tried ramming the pruning shears just above the eyeholes, but when that didn't work, she wound up smashing it repeatedly with a hammer. It took fourteen minutes of banging for it to crack even a little. Natalia really had no upper body strength.

The dogs woofed and fought to lick the iron-rich blood from Natalia's skin. Like they wanted to eat her.

Natalia knew that right now she looked like a cold-blooded, crazed murderer. But Amber had been dead upon her arrival back to the Podere. She was simply trying to salvage her young life, and prolong it. She wanted her alive, not disgraced. This was to give her a legacy, not desecrate her body.

She needed her brain because—if she was going to eat any parts of Amber, it had to be her heart, belly, and her brain. She knew that in her bones. That's what made sense in her own body. Her brain craved closeness to Amber's. Perhaps in search of some sort of assurance she had done the right thing. Each vicarious memory summoned into Natalia's own working mind meant a kind of relief, validation.

She brought the dirtied hammer, pruning shears, and head cracked open back inside to the kitchen.

She soaked Amber's brain in water, hoping it would clean off any remnants of skulldust. She set the timer for an hour.

In the meantime, she took the sheet pan from the oven.

She cut through skin, and used her hands to nibble at the meat, getting thrown off by the boniness of the hands and feet. She ate the butt meat, which was tender and perfect, but found the fat there and on the breasts too pure for straight consumption. She should have used it in the bone broth for flavor, she realized too late. She tried eating Amber's pelvis, but when she held it to her mouth, it felt like a violation, so she stopped, kissed it, and left it with the other parts too private for proper burial.

She placed the dishes' remainders into a grocery store bag, which she rested in the sink.

Amber's phone lit up and vibrated. It wouldn't stop. Natalia grabbed it and dropped it as quickly as she'd picked it up. Charlie was calling her. She knelt down to the floor to retrieve the phone, ablaze with his name.

"Charlie?" she whispered.

"Amber. What the fuck?"

"Uh—" She realized the pitch of her voice had crept up just slightly— and was her accent subsiding, or was it just the bad service of this international call?

"Can we talk about this without you threatening me?"

"I'm sorry?" Natalia said, not sorry at all, just confused.

"I feel weird about what happened with us, too, you know."

"I—"

"It wasn't—we were both—if anything, I was—I was too drunk,

too," he said.

"Look," Natalia began.

But he didn't want to hear her, "Amber," Charlie said.

"You fucking—backpfeifengesicht!"

"What?" He said, stupidly.

"You fucking murdered her," she said.

"I—what are you talking about?"

"That's none of your stupid business, you cunt. You murdered—"

"Whoa. Who the fuck are you? What are you saying?"

"You're a fucking a rapist-murderer and you make me want to believe in God, because at least then I'd know you would rot in hell," Natalia said, and then she hung up and she could breathe again. There was nothing more to say to him. He couldn't hurt her any more. She could breathe without thinking about the air in her lungs. Thinking about her lungs made breathing hard again, because she remembered eating Amber's.

Natalia checked Amber's texts and read what she had texted Charlie. She wished she could disappear him from the world, and have kept Amber with her instead. It was so supremely unfair that in this lifetime, he'd won. And there was nothing she could do that would satisfy this cosmic injustice. No email or phone call that would even begin to make any of this okay. Ruining Charlie's life wouldn't help Amber. Not now. Natalia was the only person left who could help Amber. She had listened to her and believed her. She wished should could break Amber's phone and break Charlie. Crush his heart and his windpipe.

She separated the lobes of Amber's brain by first removing her central cortex, then poached it for just over three minutes, so they became firm.

Vegetable oil in pan, filled high. Her body was made of oil and Amber now. It came to a splattering sizzle. Burned her hand. Brains coated in an egg broken and beaten, then mixed with flour. She fried each lobe, flipping them once their oiled side got golden. Sprinkled with salt.

Lobe-by-lobe, she ate, cherishing each dank and delicate bite. Each bite, brought something new and all-consuming. The mood ring Amber wore in sixth grade. Her favorite spot in the park. The Panic Attack on 57th Street. Cafe Sabarsky. Mamma Mia! tbh writing emails out of indignation is my kink. Mystery of Love. She he e could see how ow o far fa a she he e could break them hem em e before they hey he e had ha a lost all meaning. Sloths are real. Grimes looks like that?? Getting into college. Her high school physics teacher. Her thirteenth-birthday party. Plato's symposium coming to Starz next fall !!! Mood Ring in Bushwick with Emma and Allie. Mint chocolate tea at Alice's Tea Cup with angel wings and glitter stuck in her hair. Mamma Mia: Here We Go Again! Natalia. Natalia. Natalia. Natalia. Natalia. She remembered and saw Natalia. Searching Natalia. Natalia Maloof and Natalia Houghton. Natalia Meloni with the blonde hair. Natalia's Pizzabar in FIDi. Natalia. Natalia and The Girls. Natalia's brain. Natalia's body. Natalia's cure.

Natalia was blushing by the time she finished. She spent the next few hours scouring the house for evidence, and wiping them from sight. Bleaching, cleaning, retrieving, whatevering.

She waited till dark to take Amber's remains with her to bury somewhere in the woods of Parco Naturale Regionale di Bracciano Martignano. Walking down the main road, she felt so alone. The town was so small and quiet. No cars in sight.

The bones were still heavy, but without the meat that makes up a living person, it was a lot more manageable to carry than before, when she had to carry her down to the kitchen. Natalia had divided the weight between two bags: skull in the backpack; bones in the tote bag. All of Amber was wrapped gently in hand-knit blankets. Alessandra would surely notice their absence. She had packed too many gardening tools, as who knew what she would find beneath the surface, when she began to dig.

She walked past the picnic tables, deeper into the wooded territory. Searching for someplace hidden, but fitting. She found a spot with a nice view of the lake, and decided that was where she would dig. The dirt was rich, but thirsty. It needed a good rain. Not too many rocks to dodge. But still. The dogs had not done much damage to the bones. They were still so large and hard to hide. She couldn't get them six feet under if she wanted to be done by sunrise. Three feet would have to do.

Water and salt spilled from of her pores and her eyes as she dug the grave.

Natalia spent her last day in Trevinano bleaching everything she could again and again, cleaning the Podere over and over again, hoping to wipe away any memory of this. She packed up all of their belongings, and threw away whatever she couldn't fit. She had told Luca to make arrangements for someone to care for the dogs. She ate Amber's partially-cured belly for breakfast, alongside her coffee with milk. Everything else felt trivial and irrelevant. A car delivered her to the Orvieto train station. From there, it was about three hours to Rome.

She ran through her own recollection of her time in Trevinano. Her first nights there before Amber's arrival—and then Amber. She tried to remember everything they had talked about, consumed, felt. Remembering everything two ways was impossible. One memory eroded the other, rewrote it.

She wanted nothing more than to fall asleep on Amber's shoulder. Instead, she listened to *Mystery of Love* on repeat, because what else was left?

She transferred trains in Rome, then arrived at the airport. No checked bags, and security didn't flinch when she used Amber's passport as her own.

On the plane, she slept and dreamt of grey.

She awoke to flight attendants coming around with warm croissants, burnt coffee, water, and orange juice. The thought of food made her ill.

Her mind was broken. Breaking. Aching.

Home. She he had ha to get et home.

She was going home.

Fingers-to-neck, Natalia felt for her pulse. She felt sick. Queasy.

Her stomach gasses rose to her throat, tempting her with the possibility of sweet release. Her body was ill, she had to throw up. She couldn't throw up. All this life was stuck inside her. It lived in her body and would never escape it. She felt disgusting. Like she was sweating up, like she was boiling and the water inside her was oozing out of her pores. Like she was being cooked alive, her brain was frying, her ears were ringing.

The plane landed and she pulled herself together. Got through customs, into the city.

Just saw two ants drown together in my bathtub and it reminded me of us: a love story.

— Melissa Broder

This haze of delayed processing and remembering left Natalia cloudy. She followed her gut and wound up outside Central Park by where Amber grew up. She couldn't keep focus. Her mind pulled in too many directions, making her dizzy and tired. When she resigned herself to a meditative non-presence, she tasted Amber's iron and blood in her mouth.

She couldn't live like this. Knowing what she'd done—what she felt she had to do. What she felt Amber had wanted her to do. She couldn't stop remembering. The taste of Amber's flesh. And everything it lived through.

She tried to stay focused on the concrete. Focused on the traffic: people and passing cars. Natalia had never been to New York before, but she recognized places. Not tourist attractions or major landmarks—she recognized Amber's therapist's office. Her favorite park bench. Her apartment building. They felt like frozen memories, etched into her brain.

Natalia swallowed some pooled-up spit and sat down on the park bench when she realized it wasn't the traffic she was seeing, it was just the color purple. Not quite haze, more a mist. Maybe a state of pure empathy. She was remembering what her own body had never known.

She had to stop herself or she would lose herself.

She blacked out.

When Natalia came back to the present, it seemed hours had passed. She felt she'd lived through Amber's whole experience of the past week or so. She even saw all the cost-comparing flight content she read, which led to Amber's flight to Italy.

The sun had swapped favor from one horizon for the other. Her stomach rumbled again, mad at her, and begged her to listen.

"I don't know what you want," she said, "I gave you all of me." Which was true.

She walked down Central Park West, not sure where she was headed.

A homeless man said to everyone who wouldn't listen, "I'm so fucking hungry, I can't even think. If any of you have any munchies or something, just any munchies or something. Or sixty cents. I just need sixty cents and I can get a dollar slice. Sixty cents, that's it. I'm not trying to swipe. God, I would tear up a slice right now. Just sixty cents. Seriously, no one??? You can't give me sixty cents? If you all gave me one cent, goddammit, why can't—I just want one slice of pizza. This should be illegal. I'm so hungry. I'm so hungry. I'm so fucking hungry. You're all so greedy. My stomach hurts. I can't think. I feel fucking crazy, man!" He fell to the ground in front of a Waffles & Dinges cart. Someone called the cops.

She he should've gotten help.

She was shaking and sobbing now, forgot she could be perceived.

"Miss, are you okay?" someone asked her.

"I wish we were like the stars," she said.

The stranger smiled before he left. He looked so scared.

Natalia decided to cross through the park. She headed east.

When she was little, her mother used to warn her that sex made you vulnerable because someone would be inside you, which terrified her until the day she had sex and she saw the face of Elias as he came. His face twitched, eyes closed, and he bit his lip. He couldn't lie about how he felt.

Natalia loved this power of absorbing external limbs and seeing unfiltered reaction. Dicks, fists, fingers, even feet. She would put anything in her, if only to have it for a little while longer. It made her feel immortal, or, at least, beyond her own mortality. All her affairs became horcruxes—she had never read Harry Potter. Of course, Amber had—their visits inside of her bound them to her forever in this unspoken way. Perhaps this was her strange addiction. Human consumption or absorption, of any variety. She was a parasite, and wanted to be dead.

She made it to the other side of the park and kept walking. It was sticky and humid. She sweated through her shirt.

Her vision became fuzzy and she lost control over her own body.

She passed by a sign that read "Amber" on Third Avenue in front of what appeared to be a restaurant. Her insides froze and she walked faster. Was she hallucinating? She was running now. Everything became purple, and it became hard for her to register reality. Her senses were overloaded with information, perceived by two minds in one body. She vaguely felt herself slowing her pace to catch her breath, making a phone call, and getting into a cab.

When she came back to presence, she was outside of an apartment, no longer in Manhattan. She held down the buzzer, impatiently waiting for someone to answer.

"Come on up!" A voice said to her while the door BRANG and released its lock. She pushed it forward, and entered the building. She had been there before—well, one of them had.

Up the stairs, flight after flight. Too many flights of everything these days. Out of breath. She knocked on the door. "I'm here," she said.

"Ahhh!!! Amber!! Come in. It's unlocked." Natalia entered, and saw Emma, brewing tea. Without looking up, Emma said, "I'm making tea."

"I've missed you." Natalia's voice had become eerily similar to Amber's.

Emma looked up to see Natalia, and her face flickered with confusion. "Who are you? I thought you were—." Emma's voice trailed off.

"It's been a lifetime," Natalia said, nearly crying.

"Who are you?" Emma repeated.

"I'm Amber's—we were in Italy."

Emma's face flooded with fear. "What happened?" Emma said.

Natalia just cried, wanting to explain everything—to show Emma the connection that brought her here. But she couldn't get the words out.

"Is she okay???" Emma said.

Natalia shook her head, unable to speak. Shivering with fear and love and guilt. Emma forgot the tea, and embraced Natalia. They hugged each other, crying and mourning the Amber who used to be. The purple haze kept threatening to return, to cloud their clarity of mind, dragging them forward in time.

On a train rushing past stops they'd like to visit. She forgot where she was going. If she was heading anywhere. She missed cradling Amber's head in her hands. She remembered her eyes, staring at her.

She found herself on her doorstep. A dead child delivered by the death stork.

Unlocking the door with her usual pair of keys, when her heart stopped. She could feel the pulse of the life in the apartment. The weight of Amber's identity threatened to unleash with the opening of the door. She couldn't push it open. It was too heavy, the weight of it. She felt it in her chest, in her heart. Was this death chasing her? She had to run. Away from it, from the memories. She couldn't go back. Amber was dead, and so was Natalia. They were one—but their togetherness negated their own individual personhood. They were a shadow. A carcass of memories.

Down the stairs, out of the building, through the park, down the streets. Her mother's eyes haunted her. Stared at her through the movie theatre of her mind. She needed to escape her judgment. She was so afraid. Foot after foot, step after step, she kept going and going. She couldn't stop moving. She had to keep going forward. If she kept going, they could never catch up with her. They couldn't ask questions. She didn't need anyone questioning them. Out of breath, brain throbbing, body rebelling, she wound up outside Smith & Wollensky's, with a hunger she hadn't felt since—well, since their sacred union.

Without so much as opening the menu, they ordered themselves a water, coffee, and steak—rare.

The waiter brought out a steak knife. *Bread knife, carving knife, chef knife, boning knife, utility knife, filleting knife, steak knife, paring knife.*

She remembered cutting into Amber's heart—perfectly medium rare. She had used a steak knife to cut in. She'd never tasted anything so rich and tender. Her stomach throbbed, but not in ache or pain—with life. It beat with Amber's heart, reunited in a body alive.

Her phone RANG. BRRRANG. BRAAAAAAANG. BZZZZZZZZZZ. BLEEEP.

When the steak came, Natalia nearly gasped aloud with relief.

Amber didn't believe in free will. She believed in neurotransmitters and biological reactions that led to patterned behavior. She was nothing if not her body, and her body was evidence.

Her body was her truest work. She was Shelley, the doctor, and his monster.

Her stomach was queasy, there's too to o much inside.

She knew what to do.

She picked up the steak knife.

Stuffed like a pig pi, full of herself.

The only way to fill the hole in her heart.

Herself inside and an a she he can't get her he e out.

Only way to become one with her, truly.

She he e wanted to get out.

The way to become whole.

She he e wanted to come com co o up and an a get et e out.

How ho o did she he let et e her he e die di i?

She he was as gagging. Reflux was reflex.

She wanted to go back.

BRRRANG. BRAAAAAANG. BZZZZZZZZZZ. BLEEEP. Amber called her.

> been bee be e so bad ad a
> been bee be so good goo go o
> ust jus us u guilt and an a
> you'll forget

all the he e things thing thin

> We've fucked each other
> up and an a over
> There's no place lace ace to run un u
> And an a now ow o that hat ha a I've come com co o
> I'm done one on e

She took the steak knife to her plate, placed her left hand on the steak, and bit her lip as she sawed into her fingers. She was crying.

"I love you, I love you, I love you," she whispered till the words became soundless. Blood spattered and stained the white linen tablecloth. She picked her pointer finger up with her fork and swallowed it whole—bones, blood, and flesh.

Her heart RANG. BRRRANG. BRAAAAAANG. BZZZZZZZZZZ. BLEEEP.

Her mind had broken, but she needed some of her body to be inside of her, too. Together with Amber. She felt in her bones, she had to put herself through her own mouthhole to make them one whole. She took another bite of her finger, just as her waiter came around to check in on her steak. This time, she bit down. Chewing it, not letting it slip by like a hard pill she had to swallow, but forcing herself to feel the crunch of each tiny bone. The brine of the blood. The crackle of each vein. Her supple skin. Her saliva wouldn't dissolve it. The finger bud was too alive. Her mouth felt dry. Swallowing became more difficult—the finger caught between her mouth and throat—nearly choking her. She tried to force it, sipping water to help it down.

"How is it?" the waiter said, all smiles until he saw what she'd done. He became a ghost.

But before he could do anything—before anyone could do anything to keep them apart—Natalia pushed the steak knife through her heart.

Acknowledgments

First and foremost, I'm grateful to Grey Borders for believing in me and in this book. I'm forever indebted to Jordan Fry and Priscilla Brett for publishing my debut novel.

Thank you to the following people, without whom this book would not have been possible: my mother, for showing me how to find strength in vulnerability, teaching me how to cook, and for reading every single iteration of this book. My father, for catching my tpyos and for supporting me. Sammy Rosie Robinson, for being the best dancer—and the best dog. Larry Salz, for always trusting my voice. Sam Lipsyte, for giving me the push to keep going and delve deeper when I needed it—and for giving me the encouragement when I needed that, too. Hilary Leichter, for the Netflix show *Diagnosis* and for all of your help from the very start. Everyone who saw sections of this piece in workshop, as well as Dorla C. McIntosh for keeping the Columbia Creative Writing Department running. Alessandra Saggin and Luca Napolitano, for inadvertently sending me down this rabbit hole via Italian class. Podere Orto, for forcing me off the internet and into the depths of my mind. Amanda Kramer, Amanda Montell, David Iserson, Joey Soloway, Marie DeNoia Aronsohn, Mo Crist, Polly Silverman, Rachel Gould, Sara Benincasa, Susanna Fogel, Tyler Shields, and Zara Lisbon for the ongoing inspiration and for helping me to develop my own voice. Adam Glusker, Ali Saadeddine, Cody Benfield, Courtney Fulcher, Hannah Link, Jay Castro, Jesse Cao, and Michelle Chow, Thomas Wee. Kendra Epstein; Louis Schott; Monty Jackson; and Samantha, Sharon, Grant, and Liam Gillen for being like family and so supportive. Ben Gillen, for showing me what love is.

And lastly, thank you to the *Hannibal* fan pages, to Melissa Broder for making the *Eating Alone in my Car* podcast, and to everyone who followed my fake Twitter.

Emily Robinson is a writer, actor, and director living in Los Angeles. She holds a degree in Creative Writing from Columbia University.

Instagram: @EmilyRobinson

Consumed

By Emily Robinson

Copyright © 2023 Grey Borders Books

All Rights Remain With The Author

ISBN: 978-1-989119-42-6

Edited by Jordan Fry and Priscilla Brett

Layout and Design By P. Brett

Hardcover Editions Bound By Hand By P. Brett

Published By Grey Borders Books

Niagara Falls, Ontario, Canada

First Edition Hardcover October 2023

First Softcover Edition October 2023

WWW.GREYBORDERS.COM